AN ALTCOIN
TRADER'S HANDBOOK

NIK PATEL

CONTENTS

ACKNOWLEDGEMENTS

I would like to extend a special thank you to the following individuals, for their continued support for this book throughout the writing process:

J. Brown, Conor, Chris Barrera, Mark, Nate Murray, Carlos, Christian Larco, Jean-Philippe Langevin, Kuba Jeziorny, Jesse, Brian Nau, Makyla Deleo, Ramtin Neydawood, Alexander, V. Callanan, Rich from The Block Street, S, Ganske, Timothy Yu, Stephan Mauermann, Kingshuk Mukherjee, Florian Maier, Ramesh Kumar, Davide Rivola, Timothy Nakashima, R. Perrott, R. Frazer, K. Rak, Aaron Alsop, Yihsuan Chou, Nicolas Mhd, Matthew Nice, Jens Andersen, Hank, Mo Almasri, Sven Luiv, Bradley Libson, Joe Allis, Mark Adams, Anson Lee, D. Kaminski, S. Fitzgerald, James Russell, Stephen Diplock, Andrea, Joe Marciano, K. Kristiansen, Pedro Herrera, Jure Posel, Andy Kim, Tonis, E. Laing, Eric Gilbert Williams, P. Wojtyna, Dominic Reeves, David Pa, Rodrigo Nicolas Nasif, Zerosumfame, Nicholas Parker, C. Weiscop, Su Augusta, Silov, Stasys Bielinis, Kenn, Nicolas Valente, David M, Matt R, Bud Hennekes, Saagar Raju, Fahim Sidek, John Gastaldo and Peter McCormack.

Note: For those who'd like to see full-colour versions of the charts depicted in the book:
http://s000.tinyupload.com/index.php?
file_id=43368423681073584584

PART ONE: A MEMOIR

Chapter One

IN THE BEGINNING

Though, I would imagine, many readers of this book will have become aware of it via Twitter, and thus will already know a little bit about me, I feel that a little background information wouldn't go amiss for those who have not yet had the (dis)pleasure. Dad-like sense of humour aside, I am a full-time writer, speculator and advisor, all within the emerging world of cryptocurrencies, cryptoassets, altcoins or whatever else one wishes to name them. I like to use *cryptosphere* as an all-encompassing term for the goings-on in this weird and wonderful space, though, for the purposes of this book, I am expressly concerned with the novel financial market that has developed around the birth and growth of the technology, as well as the plethora of life-changing opportunities it has brought with it. Prior to my involvement in the space, I had little to no trading or investing experience – I was barely eighteen years-old –

and it was the excitement I found towards what I had accidentally stumbled upon that consumed me and led me to where I am today. I hope to impart at least a little of that excitement in the pages of this book, alongside all of the knowledge and experience I have amassed over the last five years on the topic of profitable altcoin speculation. These markets truly are unlike those of traditional finance (and, having also spent some time speculating in those, I can tell you that these are far more-readily grasped), and it is the first time in my admittedly short lifetime that I have come across such an abundance of opportunities for those with little initial capital, as I myself began with. I'll spare you any further preamble, and begin... well, where it all began.

Late 2013:

I began my journey when and where many others in this space seem to have began theirs: Dogecoin. It was around Christmas when I first came across the subreddit for Dogecoin, and I have little to no recollection of how I got to it. What I do remember is that I had never heard of Bitcoin prior to this point, let alone any other so-called 'cryptocurrencies'. I was newly-eighteen at the time, and, as such, cryptocurrency was an entirely non-existent concept in my life – my teenage years were more preoccupied with the discovery of binge-drinking than groundbreaking financial technology.

Stumbling upon this subreddit swiftly changed that, and I found myself caught up in a strange world comprised almost exclusively of memes, amused more than seriously interested, at this point. There was no tip-bot back then, and I had no idea how one might buy any Doge, and thus I followed the advice in one particular thread, downloaded the Windows wallet and created my very first cryptocurrency address. If I'm honest, I had absolutely no idea what any of it meant, but I do know that it was an indescribably enjoyable experience despite that.

Shortly after this, I happened upon the subreddit /r/dogecoinbeg (a page where strangers asked for free Doge from other Reddit users) and got to work. Yes, me – an eighteen-year-old – asking strangers on the internet if they could spare some digital change. What an odd time to be alive. It may well have been one of the weirdest moments in my life; that first exchange between myself and another Reddit user, asking for my very first coins.

But damn, it was weirdly a lot of fun. I couldn't tell you precisely why, but I remember feeling that, despite all of the surface-level silliness, this mechanism of exchange – and the idea of a 'digital currency' – was one of great significance. I was instantly hooked. My evenings began to be spent poring over the Dogecoin subreddit, growing my miniscule stack of coins via e-begging, and generally immersing myself in this novel world. Keep in mind, I was still unaware of much else in the cryptosphere besides the Shibes that I had grown to love. It wasn't until the turn of the year that I truly found myself involved.

January 2014:

New Year came and passed, and I remember being sat at my desk, Googling 'cryptocurrency', simply to learn a little more about what was sitting in my Dogecoin wallet. It was at this time that I recall first finding out about Bitcoin, which was then valued at around $900, and, after several hours of reading short posts and articles, I had the now near-universal realisation that this was truly a revolutionary idea. There was something about the ability to exchange value, peer-to-peer, with no central authority, that felt refreshing and necessary.

Though only eighteen, and still in college (high-school, for you yanks), I was relatively clued up on the disadvantages and disingenuousness of our current banking system, having read much on the 2008 credit crisis, and having seen the subsequent effects on both, immediate family, and the world. I knew from a fairly young age that I distrusted banks, and I held suspicion towards the notion of ever holding a vast proportion of any future savings in a bank account. I say 'future' because, at eighteen, working at quite possibly the most mind-numbingly dull part-time job ever, I was earning maybe £200 a month, at the very most. I am aware that this is, in fact, somewhat of a luxury, and certainly a first-world problem, since £200 a month in many places amounts to a great deal, but relatively-speaking, it was pittance. It provided the pocket-money necessary to waste away my weekends wasted.

But, I digress. The point is, I was certain that I did not have much faith in banks, and the discovery of cryptocurrencies sparked a curiosity within me particularly due to that. I proceeded to download the Bitcoin Windows wallet, though I had none to store, nor knew of any means by which to procure some (there was no /r/bitcoinbeg, as far as I can recall). This was the first time I came across the mechanics of the blockchain. Dogecoin had only existed a couple of weeks before I found it, and so, there simply was no blockchain to synchronise in the wallet. As somebody who was the furthest thing from technologically-literate at the time, I had no idea what was going on, thought that the wallet wasn't working, and deleted and reinstalled it expecting different results. When that little green bar reappeared, I thought it best to see if Google had a solution to the supposed problem. And, of course, there was no problem, aside from my tech illiteracy.

Ah well, I've come leaps and bounds since then, I promise. If I'm honest, I barely knew what the specs on my laptop meant, let alone what a blockchain was, and why it was taking so bloody long to synchronise. The internet is a wonderful tool during times of ignorance or idiocy. Anyway, the wallet at last synchronised, and there I sat, staring at my two open wallets: zero Bitcoin, and 12,000 Doge ($4-worth). And thus began my revolution.

(For added context, I just checked the historical snapshot on Coinmarketcap and there were only sixty-five cryptocurrencies in existence at that time, though, *at that time*, I'm sure that in itself must have seemed previously inconceivable to those who had been involved in the space for longer than me.)

Before I move on to the next stage of my journey, I'd like to mention that in January the Dogecoin subreddit had finally gotten a tip-bot. This streamlined the process of exchange and allowed for my less than a pint's worth of Doge to amass into nearly $35-worth (20,000 Doge). I know – the calculation doesn't make sense given that 12,000 Doge was only worth $4, but more on that later. Nevertheless, it was this amount that kick-started my desire to learn how to make money from cryptocurrencies.

February 2014:

February brought with it a shift in the level of my involvement in the space. I went from being somewhat of a scrounger to throwing whatever money I had to my name at it. I owned 20,000 Doge; a small amount but enough to play around with, I figured.

Via Reddit, I had discovered another newly-launched project by the name of Vertcoin. It was upon this discovery that I first had thoughts of real investment. Up until this point, remember, I had put absolutely nothing in except a little time and enthusiasm. I had perhaps £350 in my bank account from working my part-time job, and I had no financial responsibilities – rent, bills and food were covered by living at home. I came across a post in the Vertcoin subreddit explaining the potential of the coin; how, given the right promotion, its value could rise exponentially, just like that of Doge. I was drawn in, and began to have thoughts of investment. But where to begin? I knew I had the 20,000 Doge, and I knew that its value was now around $40 (I had also stumbled upon the treasure-trove that is Coinmarketcap by this point, and so, I could monitor the fiat values of the seventy-odd coins that were in existence). What I did not know existed was exchanges.

After a week of responding to posts in the Vertcoin subreddit and concerning myself with the conversation, I had picked up $12-worth of Vertcoin via tips. I subsequently happened upon and signed up for my first exchange – the mighty Mintpal. I also thought it wise to sign up for numerous other exchanges (Cryptsy and

CryptoRush come to mind), but Mintpal was the one with by far the most appealing UI, and thus, it was the one that stole my attention from the outset. It was so damn pretty to look at, I'm telling you. We don't have an exchange like it anymore. If I had to estimate, it must've been mid-February by this time. I can't recall specifics, and, thanks to the great Mintpal scam, I also have no reference point to return to for anecdotes from that time. Thus, whatever follows on the topic of Mintpal may be hazy.

Not only did I create a few exchange accounts, but, if I was to take this investment idea seriously, I would need a place to buy Bitcoin with my GBP. Enter, LocalBitcoins. LocalBitcoins was the first major fiat-to-BTC exchange open to those of us from the UK, as far as I remember, and it was the place my trading journey truly began. Risking my own somewhat-hard-earned money was a step of great significance, and undoubtedly it implied that eighteen-year-old Nik had some faith in not only the survival and growth of the space itself, but also in my own ability to actually turn a profit. That, or I was just a naive, cocky teenager. Probably the latter. I had no prior investments, nor trading experience, though my father had been trading equities for around seven years, and thus I had someone available to guide me on the fundamentals. That being said, I don't recall asking for any guidance, whatsoever – typical attitude of somebody who had yet to even finish his A-levels. I don't know if I was arrogant, ignorant, or stubborn, or a combination of all three, but perhaps asking for some help would've been useful. I don't regret not asking, of course, but more on all that later.

So, I opened up a fresh account with LocalBitcoins, eager to throw in my chump-change, though, to me, it really was a significant amount; maybe £150 – around half or more of what I had in my bank account. The process was all very simple, and by this point I had grown used to the use of wallets and addresses, and making transactions was no longer troublesome. There was a period where I expected every transaction to somehow get lost in the blockchain, and don't get me started on my first thoughts on 'unconfirmed' transactions. I bought the £150-worth of BTC, which, at $500 a bitcoin, was around 0.35BTC, if I recall correctly. Half an hour later, my Mintpal balance was 0.35BTC in the green. Furthermore, I swiftly transferred over my Vertcoin and Doge, and I immediately dumped the Doge, my thought process being that the more BTC I begin with, the more I can make. My mistake. And so begins the steep learning curve.

To give a little context before beginning this next chapter, I believe we're now late into February, and my Mintpal balance is near-0.4BTC. Sure sounds like a lot, and, in today's world, it would be. Back then? It could disappear real fast.

Chapter Two

THE GLORY OF MINTPAL

March – April 2014:

With 0.4BTC in my Mintpal account, I felt ready to tackle the challenge of finding success as a trader. The problem with that was twofold: firstly, I didn't have a clue what the fuck a trader was, and secondly, I panicked like a child swimming for the first time without armbands, trying ever so desperately to remain afloat and not sink to the bottom of the pool. But sink I certainly did.

The date was 4th March 2014, and it was when this tale began to liven up for me. The now-auspicious day was the date upon which I first created a Twitter account, under the pseudonym 'TenaciousCrypto' (utterly missing the obvious pun to be found in 'TenaciousC'). It was also on this day that I realised that my journey as an altcoin speculator was to be a long and arduous one, with no shortage of dejection and misery.

I decided to begin with what I had initially set out to do, what I had created the Mintpal account for in the very first place; buy more Vertcoin. I recall buying 0.1BTC-worth of it to add to my minute stockpile, but, before you think, 'wow, even as a newbie he was sort of managing his risk,' this was where my risk management ended. The red and green flashing lights of the exchange were bewitching, and I found myself looking at the other coins that Mintpal had to offer. This was my first mistake – a complete and utter disregard for research (as I made sure to do prior to my Vertcoin purchase) and an equivalent infatuation with what was flashing the most. I would like to take a brief moment to sarcastically applaud my younger self for making that day the worst day to-date that I have ever experienced as a trader in percentage-terms.

The coin of note was a little project named Mazacoin. They, under the guidance and leadership of a man unknown to me, endeavoured to be the first coin to liberate a downtrodden people: the Lakota Nation. And an admirable enterprise indeed it was, hooking me and drawing me in with its altruistic purpose. But, to understand fully why I decided to utilise the remaining 0.3BTC of my Mintpal balance for this particular coin, you need to be aware of another coin that garnered much attention that day.

Auroracoin was the cryptosphere's first ever airdropped coin, and a coin that is to this day remembered for its mammoth pump. I sat and watched in awe that day as Auroracoin topped out at prices close to 0.14BTC, having risen from 0.005BTC in barely a week – a 2800% return in seven days. I honestly didn't know what to think... if I could achieve similar returns on my portfolio, I would have over £4000, as an eighteen-year-old; I wouldn't need to work my uninspiring part-time job; I could buy two thousand pints of terrible cider. I was euphoric before I'd even entered a proper trade. So, having witnessed the Auroracoin highs, I was determined to have my own winner of equal magnitude. Enter, Mazacoin.

Mazacoin had been listed on Mintpal the same day as Auroracoin, but was yet to really gain traction. Despite being taken in by the premise and beguiled by the possibility of being rich (relative to others my age), I was hesitant. I waited. I waited some more, all the while watching the price rise. It was maybe 8pm by this point and Mazacoin had risen 2000% since the day before, but I figured that as Auroracoin had done 28x that day, maybe Mazacoin could still return at least a 5x from where it was. Of course, I didn't take into consideration the fact that a 5x from that price would have resulted in a 100x return on the day – a highly implausible target, even for a newbie like myself. Regardless, I finally took the plunge and bought in at 16000 satoshis, and, to my supreme delight, it swiftly moved to 18000 satoshis within half an hour of my entry. The ball was rolling, and I was ecstatic. 'This is just the beginning,' I thought to myself, expecting further gains before the night was up.

But, alas, 18000 satoshis is where my luck ran dry, and soon the price came tumbling back towards my entry. 'No worries, this is just a minor setback – there must be small dips along the way up,' I observed, remembering the Auroracoin pump. But no further upwards momentum came, and, before I knew it, Mazacoin was in full capitulation. I stayed up that whole night just watching the price sink further and further, the sick feeling in my stomach swelling: 12000 satoshis... 10000 satoshis... 8000 satoshis. The morning came and I had no idea what to do. Expecting some sort of bounce, I held on, not wishing to realise my losses, and, soon after... 5000 satoshis. I had to preserve something, else I would lose the vast majority of my entire balance, and so I sold, down 70% on my position. 0.09BTC was all that remained from that trade, and, alongside the Vertcoin that I had bought, made up the totality of my portfolio; a horrific start to my journey as a trader, and one that I will never forget.

Now, a composed, clear-headed and calculated trader would not have followed such an event with more of the same, but being the inadequate and inexperienced individual that I was, I swiftly sought to rectify my errors. Since the application of my observations from the Auroracoin pump went so well the first time, I figured I had found my saving grace when I happened upon a new country-coin around ten days later: Spaincoin. With country-coins being all the rage at the time, and expecting history to repeat itself, and to this time carry me along with it, I put the remainder of my position from the Mazacoin trade into this new opportunity.

Lo and behold, I bought too late, once again, and whilst I was desperate to recover the full extent of my losses on this trade, I had, at least, learnt one thing: do not hold onto a losing trade. Of course, the lack of nuance in this statement makes it less relevant to my trading today than it was back then, and, certainly in this industry, the contrary can be the more beneficial choice, once one has mastered the art of patience. However, as a new trader, this was a pearl of necessary wisdom, and in those early days it served me well. Preservation of capital is the goal, after all, as a trader, and the conventional advice of cutting your losses early still holds some merit in this novel and infant market.

Returning to our tale, I felt a great fear for the same events unfolding as in my Mazacoin trade, more so upon seeing price move in a similar manner from where I entered at 0.0045BTC to the euphoric-but-not-quite-satisfying-enough-to-exit highs of 0.007BTC (after all, I was down 70%, and a 55% profit was not going to cut it for me) and back down to my entry price. It was here that I realised I'd missed the mark once again, and I figured that I'd give it a little more time before exiting and preserving the tiny portfolio that remained. In that half an hour, price fell further to 0.004BTC, and I went with my instinct and cut my loss. I think I recall shedding one or two tears that night. It was tough to swallow two losses in a row, despite the second loss actually demonstrating a skill I had learned, and despite that exit saving me the despair of another -70%, as I watched Spaincoin tumble to below 0.0015BTC less than 24 hours later. There was little relief in that fact.

Now, I bet you're expecting – what with the beginning of a new paragraph and all – that some light may shine on this thus far dark tale. You would be wrong. Things went from bad to worse to abysmal shortly after the Spaincoin trade was closed, as I observed that the Vertcoin chart resembled the Mazacoin chart from two weeks ago. If I had to summarise it in one word, I would say that I felt useless. I dumped my Vertcoin, knowing full-well that I had missed the pump, though, I must say, proud of myself in some respect for spotting the similarities between the charts. This observation was key to my desire to learn more about pattern recognition and technical analysis. However, at this point, I was on three straight losses, down maybe 80% of my original balance; probably £125 of the £150-or-so that I initially invested. This loss may sound small to some in real terms, but, relatively-speaking, that was almost a month's pay at my part-time job, and the futility of my 'trading', if one could even call it that, was the cause of quite some misery.

I battled between thinking that I was never going to get any level of competence at this, taking into account how terribly my journey had begun, and thinking that, in order to get somewhere better, one must start from somewhere base. Thankfully, the latter thoughts took precedence over the former, and, had they not, I most likely would not be writing this book today. Though I'll spare you the cliché woo-woo, not only must one fail in order to become proficient at their pursuit, but one must thrive in that failure and embrace it, learning as much as is possible to learn from each and every trip-up and mistake. If it makes you feel any better about any possible mistakes you've made, it took me only one month and three trades to destroy my portfolio and have less than 20% of the original available to rebuild with. The lessons I learnt in that period were invaluable, and they allowed for a change in fortunes the following months.

Alongside all of this, though I will spare you the details, the cryptosphere itself was but a newborn at this point, and the volatility of the market was matched only by turbulence in the exchanges that hosted the markets. A now-dead altcoin exchange by the name of CryptoRush was undergoing a huge scandal, with around 1000BTC and 2500LTC 'lost' in March 2014. There were also issues arising concerning the owner of Cryptsy, 'Big Vern'. In short, scams were ubiquitous, and the space was an incessant whirlpool of fear, suspicion and euphoria. I was one of the lucky few who did not fall victim to any exchange scams that occurred during those early days. At any rate, I digress. As is evident, my initial experiences in the space were woeful, and I traded blindly, with no knowledge or skill, essentially just hoping things would go well. But, it did get better.

April – May 2014:

It was not until mid-April that I actually managed to turn a profit in anything crypto-related, besides getting tips from Reddit users. Using the steep learning curve of March, I realised that I was doing something intrinsically incorrect, and that there must be a more effective manner by which to approach what I was doing. Not only this, but I also realised that, at around 75-80% down overall, it quite literally could not get much worse.

A technique I used in that instance was one of pretence. I simply *pretended* that I never had that money in the first place, and sought to begin anew with what remained. The lesson there – and it is one that holds merit even to this day – is that, psychologically, it is much less detrimental to begin again, so to speak, than it is to attempt to recover what has been lost. Even though the goal is the same, the approach becomes different. If you take a loss, or two or three, the likelihood is that you will feel the tug of despair and you will do anything you can to rectify that. What happens next is that you revenge trade, with the primary goal in your mind being recovering your loss, and, as such, the mistakes only multiply. However, if one maintains that the balance remaining after a loss is all that was ever there, you can detach somewhat from the emotional and focus on the mechanical – that is, the strategy.

Now, this is not at all an easy thing to do. That being said, I believe that the reason many may struggle with this approach to losses is because they trade with money they cannot afford to lose. By doing so, one restricts one's potential from the outset. No matter who you are, we are all slaves to the biological and neurochemical processes of our bodies, and the emotional response induced after one loses 80% of a portfolio comprised of their life savings is very different to the response to an equal loss of disposable income. Do not disadvantage yourself by beginning your journey with money that is critical to your livelihood. I know some of you will ignore that and do as you will, and that's fine, because maybe you need to undergo the misery of such a devastating loss in order to alter your mindset, but for those of you that take on this advice, I promise you that the short-term disadvantage of starting with less money will be recompensed ten-fold in the longevity of your speculation.

Indeed, I took three terrible losses, and told myself *that* money was never there, and that the little I had remaining was all I had to begin with. The advantage that I found with this is that, instead of spending time worrying and whining about what I had lost, each following success could be seen as a real win, and the wins came hard and fast in April and May.

I utilised Twitter to great effect at this time, involving myself in as much of the conversation taking place as I could, learning about the publishing of 'coin announcements', and therefore about Bitcointalk, which became a staple point of reference from thereon. I did try my hand at getting a few bounty rewards upon finding these so-called ANNs, but I had very little to offer: I was a newbie with no development, design or translation skills. When that failed, it forced me to consider that maybe I needed to look elsewhere in order to find success. It was at this point that I thought to follow the advice (and the calls) of those on Twitter who were successfully trading the ever-present pumps. What did they have that I didn't?

I recall, in early April, there being much chatter about Blackcoin. It had launched in late February and was listed on Mintpal shortly after, but there had been little price movement on it since the listing. Having taken a brief glance at the ANN on Bitcointalk – though I had no idea whatsoever about what the details in the announcement indicated – I checked out the chart on Mintpal. 'Strange,' I thought. 'Why has *this* coin been neglected, considering the sheer volume of Twitter noise being made?' Little did I know, this was, of course, a long period of accumulation, preceding astronomical movement and one of the most fondly-remembered pumps in crypto-history. I must have realised that the chart did not yet look like any of the charts from my previous three trades, and therefore the pump had indeed not begun.

I had 0.08BTC or so left, maybe a little less, and I went **all-in** on Blackcoin at around 15000 satoshis, if I remember correctly. What followed was the most intense euphoria that I can remember feeling over the past five years. 24 hours later, I was up 100%. I debated selling; locking in profit; walking away with my first win. But, as with most, greed got the better of me. I held on, watching with childlike delight as price flew. Within 48 hours, my 0.08BTC position was resembling something around 0.32BTC. Despite putting the idea of loss-recovery out of my head from the outset, it would be a lie to say that I did not feel relieved and ecstatic that I had almost recovered my entire loss with this one trade, and yet I held on. 'Why on earth would it stop here?' I postulated.

Greed can be detrimental to the growth of your portfolio, but it can also be beneficial, depending upon your ability to utilise it effectively. Of course, I was still a complete novice at this point, with no fundamental or technical analysis to ground my greed within, and, despite the small instance of pattern recognition that I had employed before taking the trade, it was almost entirely good fortune that had made the trade a winner, and that good fortune continued, rewarding my greed.

Blackcoin, a little over 48 hours after my entry, hit 80000 satoshis, and executed my sell order, completing a 530% return for my first successful trade, and bringing the bitcoin balance of my portfolio all the way back up above and beyond what I began with, sitting at roughly 0.42BTC. I would struggle to put into words how elated I felt in that moment, and the word 'euphoria' seems much too controlled. Fireworks were firing off in my head, and I wanted nothing more than another hit of that joy. 'How was it that I managed that?'

I remember being satisfied with my chart observation prior to the entry, and feeling an unquenchable thirst for more of the same. I wanted to learn everything I could about charts and patterns and analysis, if that knowledge would bestow upon me a similar sense of delight to that which I had just experienced. And so began the summer of 2014.

May – September 2014:

It was in this three or four-month period that I experienced the real opportunity in speculating on altcoins. Twitter had begun to become a hub for crypto-related chatter, with many of today's most prominent personalities finding their feet during the summer of 2014. I had become acquainted with a number of traders on Twitter, and it was evident that this was all still an experiment, with many of us having little prior experience in trading financial markets, if any.

I couldn't tell you how it all began, to be honest, and I have no idea who the very first Twitter personalities were or how crypto-Twitter first came into existence. There were maybe 20,000 people on Twitter at the time that seemed somewhat involved or interested in altcoins, and the most prominent traders, upon my arrival back in March, had a few thousand followers. Followings, relative to today, were extremely small, and the cryptosphere itself seemed very self-contained in those days. Among the traders, there were also the 'whales'; a term I had not come across until my involvement in the space. These were generally the guys with upwards of a thousand bitcoins, who lurked behind the surface, manipulating the altcoins on exchanges and conducting the pump-and-dumps that were rife at the time. Accompanying the whales were pump-and-dump groups, whose sole purpose was to fleece unwitting market participants of their hard-earned money by buying up a significant amount of an altcoin, often conspicuously (which benefited me in the future, as I will reveal later) and then revealing that coin to their groups of sheep, who would proceed to panic-buy the coin up hundreds of percent, all the while supported by spoof buy-walls from the pump conductors, who then, upon having their sell orders executed, would pull their support and the whole thing would come crashing down, often within a few minutes. It truly was the Wild West. But it also allowed for surreal returns, and it is precisely those returns that I sought out.

Having completed my first profitable trade, and having my balance restored after the tragedy of March, the first thing I did was figure out how exactly I could profit from my future trades. 'What was it that allowed for the Blackcoin trade to be a success, whilst the previous three were such failures, aside from luck, and how could I repeat that?' I thought to myself. The one thing that stood out as a point-of-difference from my first three trades was the fact that I had spotted the accumulation range of the Blackcoin chart (though I did not know it as such, at the time) and had used that to enter, expecting the chart to follow the pattern I witnessed in Mazacoin and Spaincoin. I spent hours and hours poring over the various altcoin charts on Mintpal, and, having just finished college for summer, I had all the time in the world.

I began to recognise the cyclical nature of these charts; how coins seemed to remain within a tight range for a period, followed by a breakout from that range, and a pump ensued from there, followed by a dump back to the range it began in. In order to consolidate my observations, I did what every budding trader does – I Googled 'technical analysis', clicked on Investopedia, and studied the traditional patterns. I had absolutely no clue what the terms meant, and patterns like triangles, pennants and flags must have gone straight over my head at the time, despite their simplicity, but I do remember feeling like these patterns and movements I was reading about were manifesting on the altcoin charts, and *that* reinforced the observations I was making. I became a little more confident, and began to note down which altcoins I was recognising the formation of these patterns and cycles in. To supplement this, I would compare my observations with those of the traders I was following on Twitter, and I began to formulate some sort of strategy: I would use the Bitcointalk announcements to find out about coins, then I would search for them on Twitter to find out if people were interested in them and what was being said. This I would follow with a rudimentary analysis of the coin's chart, if it had been listed on an exchange yet. From there, I would enter, and wait for the astronomical returns to present themselves to me. It seemed a sure winner at the time, and it was, though, looking back now, I feel that had it not been for the omnipresence of altcoin pumps, I would have had half as many wins as I actually did.

The first coin I can recall trading after Blackcoin was Fluttercoin. This was very shortly after exiting Blackcoin, so I would imagine it was still April at this time. I am aware this section is centred on the summer of 2014, but this trade cemented my self-confidence, and it is a fun one to recollect, so I'm going to jump back a little before we move forward. Fluttercoin was most definitely the first coin that underwent my novice analysis, as I drew straight and squiggly lines, triangles of all sorts and an array of other traditional charting techniques. Safe to say, this was no Botticelli but I do recall it teaching me a couple of things: namely, how to actually draw on a chart (at this point, I was printing charts out and scribbling on them with my ballpoint pen), and how to spot the basic structure of a pump-and-dump cycle. Now, back in 2014, these pump-and-dumps began and ended in the blink of an eye, with two to five days being the general length of time it took to take coin X from its lows up 1000% and back down 50-70% from those highs. There was less volume in the market, and, of course, fewer market participants, so the duration of time it took to 'shake out weak hands' was minimal, and the duration of time it took to pump a coin, even less so.

I had a few friends by this time on Twitter, and the discussion on Fluttercoin was much like that of the newbies of today; predominantly that the coin was going to 'moon'. I spotted the range of accumulation after charting the coin, and my fear of being wrong led to me awaiting a breakout before entry. The breakout came hard and fast, as the coin tripled almost instantly, and I felt that I'd missed my chance for a good entry, but I expected much more from the coin. So, around 500 satoshis, I jumped in. This time – and for the first time, wittingly – using less than half (or maybe just about half) of my BTC for the position. This was my first experience with risk management, but, if I'm honest, I felt more annoyance that I hadn't gone all-in than I did comfort when the trade began to progress. I had entered the trade relatively late into the evening, and – another first – went to sleep shortly after. The sleep was turbulent, to say the least, as I woke up every couple of hours in a sweat, in eager anticipation of where price had moved, and thus the night and morning progressed.

Thankfully, the sleepless night was a positive one, as my position had doubled by lunchtime the following day, and I held on, knowing full-well from Blackcoin how hard these pumps could accelerate. The euphoria began to set in once again, as price moved from 1000 satoshis to 2000, effectively quadrupling my position, all within 24 hours. I sold, anticipating a crash, and being ecstatic with the fact that my portfolio was now sitting at over a full bitcoin. The crash came, sure enough, and this only added to my euphoria, sensing that I had sold the top and was now, of course, a god-like altcoin speculator. 'This is too easy,' I thought, as I watched the coin I had just exited retrace 50%. I *thought* I'd done the impossible – sell the top. It just so happens that I was bitterly wrong, and the market can make your 'genius' win seem a bad trade as a newbie when it blows past your sell price. A few days later, Fluttercoin was 2800 satoshis, and I had missed out on an extra 40%. This should not have mattered to me, considering how great the win was, but I was embittered by it. Looking back, I am just glad that I didn't re-enter the trade, as I see many do when their sell price is surpassed. In all honesty, the embitterment didn't last very long. I guess I was just annoyed I didn't get as much out of the winning trade as I could have, but I did feel a lingering sense of self-confidence in my abilities after that trade.

The trade that followed these two early wins came in early May, though that period is hazy, and I may have missed a trade or two in between. Regardless, the next trade I clearly recall was another huge winner for me, and preceded the most iconic pump in crypto-history, or at least in my memory. The coin was a new addition to Mintpal, by the name of Cinni, and it is a coin that is no longer around. In fact, it was even delisted from Coinmarketcap, and I have had to look through the historical snapshots provided by the website of that time in order to refresh my memory about many of the details. Cinni was the first coin that I remember having a huge buzz about it on Twitter. Everybody was talking about it, and many bought as soon as it was added to Mintpal. The hesitancy in me was still apparent, and that was not an approach I went for, instead opting for a similar approach to the Fluttercoin trade.

After a week or so of the coin being listed, I could recognise that it was trading within a range from which it would later break out. This time, I wanted to risk buying within the range, and to compensate for the extra risk, I do remember 'only' putting in half of my portfolio again. To be honest, I can't actually remember whether this was to compensate for the additional risk, or because my other half of the portfolio was tied up in a coin or two that I cannot remember, but I do know it was around 0.6BTC that I put into Cinni around 10000 satoshis. For the first time, I had to experience the itch of sitting on your hands for a while whilst price lingered around the accumulation range. I had always bought post-breakout, and I was unsure whether I liked the waiting. Remember, newbies, that patience is the one thing that is utterly unteachable, and only manifests through experience. Of course we want our trades to take off instantly – greed enforces this desire within us. We want quicker trades to reinvest more immediately and make even more money. But, if we have the patience (and the conviction in our analysis and ability), as I found out, the itch of the wait is more than made up for by the better pricing.

Cinni hadn't actually traded much below 6000 satoshis, so my entry was barely more than 50% above the very lows, which, in this market, was nothing. A couple of days passed and price was still hovering above 10000 satoshis. A couple more days passed, and price had finally begun to move, surpassing 20000 satoshis and doubling the value of my position. I was more wary on this trade than previously – I was aware that the amount of bitcoin I was trading was getting larger, and the fiat profits were of course getting larger alongside that. I waited a little longer before executing my sell, and bagged a 2.5x on the trade; a smaller percentage gain than my recent wins, but the largest win in BTC that I had experienced so far. The issue here was that I had gotten a taste of the 'larger money', and so, when I saw price hit 30000 satoshis, I re-entered the whole amount. 1.5BTC back in at 0.0003BTC... what a stupid idea. Price swiftly topped out at 37000 satoshis and crashed back to my entry. 'Do I stay in or exit and retain my profits?' I asked. Greed got the better of me, and in I remained. This, however, did not last very long, as price continued to fall, albeit only 10% before I aggressively market-dumped. I lost 0.2BTC or so of my profits because of the latter half of that trade, and it tarnished my positive experience. Whilst, of course, it was still a win, giving back your profits is detrimental to one's mindset.

And, though confident, I was again feeling the necessity to second-guess myself when my next large trade presented itself. That trade was none other than the infamous Darkcoin, or Dash, as it is known today, and if I had to pick one pump in my experience that has stuck with me as the most iconic, formative and emotional, it is inarguably that one. To give further context, my portfolio at this point was maybe a little under 2BTC, and, in the three months that I had now spent within the cryptosphere, I had yet to discover a coin that offered something **new**.

Darkcoin brought anonymity to the table for the very first time in a serious way, and the effect that such a development had was tremendous. Fundamental analysis had largely evaded me, partly because, up until this point, there was nothing truly innovative that I had stumbled upon – most new coins were just Bitcoin with different parameters and possibly new algorithms. However, anonymity; even I recognised the significance of that. As far as I can remember, the tech was not at the level of some of the anonymity protocols that have been developed since, but Darkcoin paved the way for all of it. I recall it being added to Mintpal in March, and talk had been slowly escalating on Twitter. It was one of those situations where everybody knew this coin was going to pump, but nobody could tell when. The indicators for a large-scale pump were all there: new tech; social media buzz; more volume pouring into Mintpal. What followed was unprecedented.

Price had lingered within an accumulation range for far longer than other coins that I had traded, between around 0.001BTC to 0.0015BTC for around six weeks, and from this the assumption was made that all of us on crypto-Twitter were in for the greatest pump to-date. I think I must have entered with roughly a full bitcoin (50-60% of my portfolio), mostly driven by the thought that this was the trade I could not miss, and that could truly make me some significant money. I, unfortunately, did not enter during this long accumulation phase, as much of my bitcoin was tied up (predominantly in the Fluttercoin and Cinni trades), but I did manage to get in as the breakout began, almost immediately after exiting my Cinni position. The entry was around 0.005BTC, which was already 3x from the lows, but, fast-forward two weeks and it was a stellar price. I did envy those who got in sub-0.002BTC, but this was the first trade in which I actually felt the tingling of euphoria from the very outset. It is a strange feeling to have; the expectation of certain success. Of course, with the experience I now have, I am aware that success in this space is **never** a certainty, but I would be being dishonest if I didn't mention that early ecstasy.

Sure enough, price began to move skyward a few days later, and the level of volatility was such that I had never experienced before. The market-maker was shaking the tree at every possible opportunity, and I found myself selling and re-entering multiple times over the course of a few days, sometimes increasing my position by achieving a lower re-entry, and sometimes vice-versa. In all honesty, the ride was an emotional roller-coaster from the beginning, and the joy of exiting at 0.013BTC after the first leg up was equalled by the misery of buying 0.012BTC just before price dumped down 20%. This caused me to panic-sell, and, of course, was followed by price jumping back up above the local high of 0.015BTC. This was my first experience actively day-trading a position, and it proved to be far more difficult than the simple one-click buy and sell trades that I had been making thus far. Safe to say, I re-entered as new highs were made, as the enthusiasm on Twitter became more and more palpable. Price dumped again, but this time I held on, recognising the same patterns I saw on the previous dump, and thus identifying this move as a shakeout. My strong hands were rewarded, as a few more days passed and price hit new highs of 0.023BTC. I exited my entire position, thrilled beyond belief at the fact that, over the course of the last three months, I had now seen my portfolio value move from 0.4BTC down to 0.08BTC and up to 3.6BTC as of this exit. Price continued to move up to where it eventually topped out at 0.028BTC, 80x from the coin's lows, and 25-30x from its accumulation range, but this was irrelevant to me. In truth, I felt godly. 3.6BTC at that time was around $2000, or £1200; more than ten times my original investment.

Chapter Three

LUCKY OR GREAT?

May – September 2014 (continued):

The summer had now well and truly come around and I had finished my A-level exams, finally giving me the freedom to focus 24/7 on trading. My conviction was such that I knew I did not want to trade as a career, but I was acutely aware of the immense opportunity in the space, which left me feeling as though I would be a fool to not focus 100% of my time on altcoins whilst I could. I had three months or so to kill until my English Literature degree was to begin at the University of York, and my expectations – predicated on the previous months of trading – were that I could successfully put a dent in the exorbitant tuition fees if I could replicate my returns with the balance I now possessed. Spoiler: I more than replicated those returns, but the following months were not without their fair share of despair.

However, before we move forward with our story, I would find it impossible to write up a memoir that excluded undoubtedly the most memorable scam in crypto-history, and one that ultimately ruined many prominent figures in the space at the time. The scam, of course, was that of Zetacoin. The happenings of this debacle occurred alongside much of what I have relayed thus far, and did not come to their conclusion until towards the end of summer.

The story began in the first week of April, when sudden price movements began to draw much attention to the coin. There was an idiosyncratic buzz beginning to form – the like of which I haven't seen since – about this one particular coin that many were going so far as to hail the next Bitcoin, if not a coin that would eventually surpass it. As I say, price in early April was at its lows of around 1000 satoshis, before sudden and forceful movement pushed it up well above 4000. Chatter on Bitcointalk, alongside the cryptic, mysterious postings of our villain, @bitcoinsachs, formed the fuel for discussion. Rumours began to surface of all sorts: the adoption of Zetacoin as a national currency; the integration of Zetacoin with a debit card; major business partnerships in China. The list goes ever on. The absurdity and extremity of these rumours only served to boost price, as the coin soared above 9000 satoshis.

I had paid relatively little attention to the coin during this time, but could not escape the conversation on Twitter. There were many people doting on the teasing posts of the major figures behind Zetacoin, and a game ensued to solve the mystery of a pending announcement. The words of the immortal Konen were scrutinised incessantly, as the whole of crypto-Twitter searched for a clue. Then, quite suddenly, price began to tank, as high-volume selling drove the coin back below 4000 satoshis. Amateur detectives began investigating via the Bitcointalk thread, finding many of the top wallets distributing their positions. A conspiracy awoke. However, these findings did little to halt the cascade of believers, and, before long, I myself found it difficult to resist the promise of untold riches.

Thoughts along the lines of 'imagine if you could turn back time and buy Bitcoin at below $1; Zetacoin is your time-machine' were rife, and the mysteries only seemed to deepen. A trend of pre-announcement announcements was born, and small teasers were fed to us like sweets to Hansel & Gretel, fattening us up to be later consumed. I foolishly succumbed, and, with whatever BTC wasn't in positions at the time, began to slowly accumulate a bag, worrying not about short-term volatility, as I told myself, 'this is my long-term hold.' A couple of days passed by and the rumours were swiftly narrowed with a post by Konen that foretold of a 'real world business in Kenya and Tanzania who will use Zetacoin as a full payment option.' So, all the other rumours were swept aside and those of us involved (though I was skeptical) began to attempt to unearth anything that pointed towards a partnership in Africa. Bitcoin Sachs made it clear that the announcement could only be made by the partner themselves, and so began the awaiting of so-called 'Holy Week'.

Amongst all of this, a PDF file was circulating, written by 'the real ZET whale', which outlined what it considered to be irrefutable proof of the partnership of Zetacoin with M-Pesa, the largest mobile payment processor in Kenya. The PDF did little except cause further price volatility and fuel the ongoing debate of whether this was all too good to be true and that the space was being duped, or whether this truly was an opportunity like that of buying Bitcoin shortly after its inception. Tweets from Konen himself began to pop up, documenting his journeys to Kenya, but delays in communication and the prolonged announcement became fuel for those that doubted the project to gain more traction.

To combat this, there was more investigation by the amateur detectives of Bitcointalk, and distinct changes were found in the M-Pesa code that possibly indicated the integration of a cryptocurrency. The plot thickened. Members of the Zetacoin team themselves got in touch with a senior journalist, working for *Fast*, asking him to cover the whole story and giving a false air of legitimacy to the goings-on. One aspect of the situation I remember particularly amusingly is that of the wave of ambiguous, often nonsensical or meaningless 'insider info' being circulated on Twitter: the insiders had knowledge from other insiders that yet more insiders had heard from the true insiders (who had spoken, of course, to the team themselves) that Holy Week was upon us. It was truly ridiculous, at times. It was swiftly pointed out that the changes in code that had been spotted were for FrontlineSMS, and not M-Pesa, and this only initiated further rumours that the partnership was with FrontlineSMS now.

The month drew to a close after more speculation than on any other coin I had ever witnessed, and yet there was still no announcement. The tale truly took a sharper turn when, in early May, news articles began to circulate internationally about mobile payments and cryptocurrency; Africa and Bitcoin; and so on, and so forth. Following this, crypto-Twitter erupted, bombarding the Safaricom Twitter account with questions about the partnership in question. And then, the obvious yet unthinkable happened: On the 5th May, Safaricom tweeted out that there was no project with Zetacoin, nor any negotiations for one. Now, one of a sensible mind would think that this would draw our tale to a conclusion, but many at the time were not of sound mind or clear thought, and though price tanked on the breaking of that tweet, there was still a rebuttal against it. Believers and key figures implored holders to keep holding, since the account manager for Safaricom couldn't possibly be aware of any internal project, or since, if he/she was aware, they would have had to sign an NDA and couldn't possibly have tweeted an affirmative to the question of the partnership. Many were so entrenched in their positions and their beliefs that they overlooked the evidence in favour of faith. I had barely flinched at the tweet, expecting something of the sort to come to light eventually, though I had internally hoped for the promised land of Holy Week. I sold most of my position, though it was a small one, at less than a 20% loss. I held a little in faith, too. Price, following this, began a long-term downtrend, eventually bottoming out in early June around 2000 satoshis.

All through this time, there was little to no communication from the leading figures behind the project, and still no announcement. Towards the middle of June, price had stabilised above 3000 satoshis, and the few strong believers remained – I myself had exited my entire position by this point, in favour of other opportunities. The buzz on Twitter was severely reduced after the Safaricom tweets, but still made itself known from time to time, and, at the end of June, once again began the cries of Holy Week, and it seemed that maybe, possibly, finally, the announcement – whatever it was – was to arrive. Price climbed all the way back up above 5000 satoshis, but it was met with deathly silence, and never again returned to those heights. From July through to the end of 2014, Zetacoin remained in a downtrend, falling below 1000 satoshis, and the despair was palpable. Konen's websites and services all shut down, and any and all communication on Kenya disappeared. Not only that, but Konen's Zetacoin addresses were spotted to be dumping. Many who had put not only their entire portfolios but also life savings into the coin were emotionally and financially broken, and thus ended the Zetacoin debacle.

After that depressing but nostalgic tale, I think it is best we return to the glories of the summer of 2014, wherein I believe I established myself as a speculator and found my niche: namely, lowcaps and microcaps. The pump that I feel cemented this was that of Piggycoin. I had spent much time studying better traders and experienced many pumps by mid-summer, and the key chart patterns I had recognised by that point were triangles. Triangles were to 2014 what cup-and-handles are to newbies today. They worked effectively and they were everywhere. My portfolio, at this stage in the story, is perhaps 6BTC, and we'll call it that for the sake of clarity, though it may have been a little more or a little less.

I had also begun to develop my own form of analysis; one that I had not seen explained in any detail elsewhere. This was orderbook reading, and, back in 2014, when the entire orderbook was viewable on all exchanges, this proved a huge advantage if you knew what to do with the information it presented. I go into the specifics of this method of analysis for many pages in the second half of the book, so I won't bore you with the details here, but just be aware that it was during this summer that everything started to come together with my analytical skills, especially when focused on so-called 'shitcoins'.

Now, I'll start by saying that, whilst Piggycoin was a shitcoin of sorts, it was actually a legitimate one, if there can be such a thing. The dev was (and is still) a perfectly amicable individual who communicated often and effectively, and consistently worked on developing the coin. There was much talk about the coin being used to introduce children to cryptocurrency, so it even had somewhat of a use-case forming. I had found the coin via Coinmarketcap, and, observing the orderbook manipulation and the long period of accumulation on the chart, I bought 2BTC-worth of the coin between 10-15 satoshis, and began posting my analysis on Twitter. What I hadn't realised was that, by this point, many more of us on Twitter had started to gain a relatively large following – a following that bought first and asked questions later. The coin shot up suddenly, perhaps even doubling after those tweets, and, naturally, later retraced to a little higher than my entry.

A couple of days passed by, and the coin again began to pick up some momentum. It seemed that not only had I got in at the very lows, but I had timed it almost perfectly. I became a most ardent advocate for my beloved shitcoin as price continued to rise and my portfolio grew to all-time highs beyond my imagination. As the data is no longer available on Coinmarketcap (Piggycoin changed its ticker from PIG to PIGGY during this period, and so, data is only available from late 2014), I can't provide a chart to illustrate the pump, but suffice to say that within a week price had popped up above 100 satoshis, and I had realised the largest win in BTC-terms of any trade I had made since the beginning. I recall this trade with nothing but fondness, and it will always hold a special place amongst my memories. In total, I think I made over 10BTC off that one trade alone, and my portfolio was sitting at an impressive (to me) 16BTC. If I had to provide one moment that I believe cemented not only some sort of reputation in the space, but also my gratitude to the opportunity given to me by crypto, it would be the moment I logged into Poloniex (yes, Piggycoin was on Poloniex back then) to find all of my sell orders had filled. 16 bitcoins was equivalent to around $10,000 back then, which, when you consider what I initially put in back in February, is no small feat. And, at eighteen years-old, it is a hell of a lot of money. Heck, even today it's a lot of money. Thoughts began to circle in my mind of being able to pay off a decent chunk of my inevitable university debt. It was a magnificent feeling, and one of relief. A few trades occurred following the Piggycoin one, but none significant enough to mention here.

However, there is one more story I would like to retell before I conclude my words on the summer of 2014. This story – and I couldn't possibly end this chapter without it – is yet another infamous scam: Uro. Now, this scam was actually rather profitable for me, so I retell this story with joy, but many suffered serious losses. Uro was the promised land Mark II, announcing itself as the first coin to be pegged to urea production. Thankfully, I did not fall for this load of horse-shit (or horse-piss, if you will), and instead saw an opportunity to profit immensely from the naivety of others. That is part of the game, after all.

I spotted a heavy and prolonged period of accumulation within a tight price range on its Bittrex chart, where it was being traded. Bittrex had become my principal hunting ground for microcap and shitcoin pumps, and the exchange was seeing daily candles that exceeded 1000%, and not infrequently. So, the potential was there for a major win. Of course, this was only complemented by the noise being generated about the project (scam) and, like an opportunistic bird-of-prey, I swooped in and took a bite out of the accumulation range. I believe my entry was around 0.002BTC, in early July, just as the scam was beginning to gain momentum and the behavioural patterns of the Zetacoin cycle became evident on Twitter. Price itself was behaving in a similar manner to the Darkcoin pump, in that moves began to unfold slowly, taking almost a week before price had broken 0.01BTC. Now, keep in mind, at this point I'm 500% up on my position, though it was only a small percentage of my portfolio – I think I put in around 0.8BTC. But, this is the moment where the likeness with the Darkcoin pump ended.

The break of 0.01BTC brought with it a flurry of chaotic buying, the like of which is difficult to forget, and price was at 0.02BTC before I could make a cup of tea. Okay, perhaps not that quickly, but it was within the hour. The euphoria was everywhere, and that was my sign to get the hell out. I dumped the lot at around 0.021BTC, cementing a 10.5x on my position... another huge win. As you can tell, I hadn't quite understood the disadvantages that could have come from holding my entire position to be sold *en masse*, but it really was that easy back then. If I'm honest, sure I had some advantage from the hours I put into research and the time I spent getting to understand the mechanics of the market, but almost anyone could have made money in that market. The difficulty came in retaining it, and that became evident in the following hours. News started to break about the legitimacy of the project, and it soon came to light that – shock horror – Uro was not actually pegged to the production of urea. Who would have known, right? Those who had been furiously buying began dumping their positions even more furiously, and price, which had gone from 0.0075BTC to highs of 0.036BTC within a few hours, now came tumbling down, back below 0.0075BTC by the morning of the next day.

These were volatile times, full of falsity and fraud and deception, but equally filled with opportunity. Despite the scams and the ever-ensuing drama, the summer of 2014 is one I recall with an affectionate nostalgia. I loved that feeling of learning something new about the markets when I knew absolutely nothing (though I am still learning today), and I especially adored the community back then. There was far less bitterness and bitchiness back then, quite frankly.

Chapter Four

THE HIATUS

September 2014 – January 2015:

By the end of summer, I was spent. I was still very much interested in the space, and still enjoying the trading, but I knew that it could not last and the emotional roller-coaster had drained me somewhat. The reason for this feeling was simply that I was aware that my skill-set was not particularly well-developed, and though by this point I had figured out how to exploit the data in an orderbook to my advantage, my general analysis beyond this was inadequate. As I mentioned beforehand, almost anybody could have made money in that market. I was fortunate to have stumbled upon and developed my own niche of analysis within the Bittrex orderbooks, and I could trade solely from those, but there really wasn't a great need for that skill when you could quite literally throw a dart at a board of coins back then and be richer by the following weekend. I wanted to develop my abilities beyond trading altcoins, and, though I remained in the space for some three or four months after summer, I had begun to scale out. This was partly because I had just started university, and was preoccupied with that, but I knew I wanted to apply myself to a market that would at least allow me a good night's sleep. There were well over three hundred alts in existence now, and, with a market that runs 24/7, the opportunity for sleep was rare.

As 2014 was drawing to its close, I had amassed a portfolio worth perhaps thirty bitcoins, from the 0.4BTC I began with; a 75x return on my investment within nine months. With Bitcoin trading at around $380 in early December, that gave me $11,000 or so, from an initial investment of what equated to $250 in February. This was incomprehensible for me back then; to be nineteen years-old with more money than anyone else I knew. I made the now regrettable but reasonable decision to cash out the whole lot into fiat, putting much of it into savings and the remainder into... my newly-opened spread-betting account. That's right. I stopped trading alts in December 2014, and turned my eye towards forex and indices. The traditional markets, I thought, would show me whether I had the ability to succeed as a trader, or whether it was merely the market that made me look like a genius in alts. It was also at this time that the Twitter handle had a change; gone was @tenaciouscrypto, @daytradernik was born. I still kept up to date with the altcoin world, and was surprised yet relieved to find that I had exited on the precipice of a major bear market for alts and Bitcoin. By January 2015, Bitcoin was trading at around $280.

February 2015:

February soon arrived, and with it came the chance to refine my abilities. During the couple of months prior, I had been playing around with a demo account on a spread-betting exchange to mixed success. The results weren't convincing, and then I happened upon the InnerCircleTrader. ICT was a trader that provided intensive online tutorials on a brand of technical analysis that I had yet to see elsewhere. The series of videos – numbering maybe twenty or even thirty tutorials, each two to three hours in length – centred on price-action analysis; a style of technical analysis that I was familiar with but that I had never seen explored and explained with such precision and depth. Long story short, (since I need not retell the countless evenings and late nights I spent poring over the material, making notes, and testing out the concepts), it appears that I had found material that seemed to work miracles in the market, comprising of concepts that, when they clicked, elevated my analytical competence to a degree that nothing else had come close to. Any material that I had experienced prior was swiftly set aside, indicators were rejected, and charts became far easier to read and understand. I dedicated myself to learning his material inside-out after the first few weeks of testing out the first of his series of tutorials; I found my trade success rate had increased greatly. This took perhaps over two hundred hours of concentrated learning, and, to-date, I have probably watched the library of videos at least three times apiece.

Now, I'm not saying that *that* level of commitment is necessary to successfully learn how to read and analyse a chart, but the more time you can commit, the faster you will become proficient, putting you at an advantage over the vast majority of traders. And, to give a quick flash-forward, I still use the concepts today in my altcoin trading, and their effectiveness has not dwindled. If anything, I find price-action analysis even more effective in crypto. However, what I found to be more significant than the understanding I gained of individual charts was the understanding of tradeable markets themselves: the macro view presented by ICT – the explanation of why specific scenarios play out time and time again – was unparalleled in its utility.

I spent the months leading up to the summer trading forex and indices mainly, with the FTSE100 and USD/CAD being the two markets I most paid attention to. In that time, I made enough money to rent out a beautiful maisonette overlooking the River Seine in Paris for part of my summer, and it was at that point that I realised that the workload of university was going to become too great to couple with the stresses of day-trading. I took a hiatus as soon as my second year of university began in September 2015, allowing myself the time to focus on uni life. If I'm honest, once that hiatus began, I barely paid attention to any market, crypto or otherwise, and it wasn't until late January 2017 that my thoughts turned to markets again.

Chapter Five

THE RESURRECTION – 2017

2017:

2017; a year unlike any other in my life thus far. January began blanketed with a series of small miseries: the heating had stopped working in my student house during the coldest period of the year; I had spent any money made through trading across the previous three years on paying for university, and I was around £800 into my £1500 overdraft on my bank account; the workload for my dissertation had begun to overwhelm me; and I was battling the indecisiveness I had towards what I wanted to do with my life, since all I knew was that I wanted to write, and that, to me, was independent of any career aspirations. Whilst I enjoyed the research and writing process that went into my dissertation on Dracula, the ten-hour study days were becoming tiresome, and I needed to do something more compelling, if only to divert my mind a little during any breaks. This, along with the fact that I didn't want to leave university with no savings, gave rise to the rediscovery of Bitcoin.

One afternoon in early February, I recall directing my browser to BitcoinWisdom, just to see where the Bitcoin price was and where it had been since I left. I figured that, at worst, returning to trading would allow me to clear my overdraft, since I knew that I most likely still possessed the skill-set. You must remember that trading wasn't something I particularly enjoyed, which is perhaps why it had slipped my mind when considering potential career avenues. Even at this point, I was not thinking about a future in trading, merely a present. It wasn't until I had the realisation that, via the financial freedom that I could possibly acquire through speculation, I would be free to pursue my writing interests unbridled by the burdens of a regular job. I digress, but the point is that I remembered that trading was something that I was good at, and something that, most importantly, was immensely profitable.

It may have been a week from that contemplative afternoon before I decided to buy some Bitcoin and return to the cryptosphere, and considering I had negative £800 in my bank account, I needed to keep some of that overdraft available for every-day living. I took around £400 of the remaining £700, logged in to LocalBitcoins and jumped in at roughly $900 per BTC. Now, I don't know whether I have uniquely good luck or that I am the messiah, but it seems to me that I left on the cusp of a long-term bear market and returned at the lows before the bull market began. I'm going to hazard a guess and say it is simply good fortune, but I could very well be the messiah...

To be honest, I didn't know where to begin. Having completed a quick look-through of Coinmarketcap, I realised I no longer recognised many of the biggest coins, and I certainly didn't remember there being so many. I figured that the best place to begin would be the two exchanges I was familiar with that were still prominent from back in 2014 – Poloniex and Bittrex. These two exchanges, which were relatively small back then, had become the kings of crypto, and the UI had barely changed at all. I rejoined crypto-Twitter and made old friends aware that I had returned. At first, I believe some people thought I had sold my account, but soon it became clear that I truly was gracing the space with my presence once again. Alright, perhaps not gracing, but certainly inundating all of your Twitter feeds with first-class shitposting. What I liked most about these early moments of 2017 was the feeling that I was starting again from scratch, and that I would be able to retest my microcap trading abilities and find out just how quickly I could turn a small amount into a vast amount. The beauty of altcoins is precisely that; the opportunity for relatively swift returns on an unparalleled scale. That £400 could quite easily clear my overdraft within a couple of trades, and it did.

Before I get into the wonder of the bull market of 2017, I think it is important to point out that I was still anonymous back then, for the most part. Sure, my Twitter handle had changed from @tenaciouscrypto to @daytradernik, but my profile picture was a Leicester City badge and I had no personal information in my bio. I made the decision almost immediately after returning to Twitter to dox myself. Honestly, I cannot for the life of me remember why this seemed like a good idea at the time – perhaps because I had relatively little to lose by doing so – but I don't regret the choice at all: there is something quite liberating, though a little scary, about shedding the mask of anonymity and embracing your real identity amongst a community still very much attached to their aliases. And don't get me wrong, I 100% understand why someone would choose to remain anonymous, more so after the hack I experienced myself. To be honest, I think part of the reason why I doxxed myself was because I felt that, if anybody really wanted to, they could find out who I was without much difficulty. Regardless, I believe that the decision to reveal who I was has actually made me feel more strongly attached to the community, since there is no cartoon to hide behind anymore – everything must be authentic. No doubt this played a part in the subsequent growth of my Twitter following.

The crypto-Twitter explosion is, in fact, a great place to begin the story of 2017. If I recall correctly, I had maybe 4,000 followers upon my return in February. Within a couple of months, this was closer to 10,000 followers (and, at the time of me writing this, it is approaching 50,000). This violent expansion of the community was unprecedented, and strongly correlated to the dramatic increase we were witnessing of public interest in cryptocurrency at the time: Bitcoin shot through its all-time high of around $1175 in late February, and with the explosive movement of price came a flood of new and curious people. Many who had never considered Bitcoin to be a viable project shifted their opinion as new highs were made, and those seeking the impressive returns came flooding onto Twitter to find out just how they could profit.

But, I had yet to make a public call. Up until mid-to-late February, I had been watching the markets silently. As I said before, Poloniex and Bittrex were my first reference points for re-syncing myself with the market. A lot had changed, as was evident by the fact that a coin needed a market cap of over a million dollars to get into the top 100. I repeat – ONE. MILLION. DOLLARS. Sounds like absolutely nothing, right? And today, that wouldn't even get you into the top 400 coins, but twelve months ago that seemed like an astronomical amount to me, relative to where the space was when I left in 2015. For context, a top 100 placement on Coinmarketcap required $115,000 in February 2015.

As a quick aside, I believe there will come a time where every coin in the top 100 is a billion-dollar network. Whether that comes in this bull cycle or following a bear market, I couldn't say.

Anyway, I was studying Poloniex more intensively than Bittrex, since it was doing more volume at the time, and I remember coming across two charts that particularly piqued my interest: LibraryCredits and Golem.

Golem had only recently been listed on Poloniex, and I remembered that new listings on large exchanges tended to pump. Not only that, but the coin itself was a token for a supercomputer project... this seemed a far-cry from the shitcoins that I was used to trading. It was trading in the top twenty coins at that point, so it was a large project already, but I felt confident that the new volume that would be brought to the coin by the listing – coupled with the impressiveness of the idea behind it – would lead to price growth. I took up my first position in over two years, entering around 2400 satoshis in late February. Thankfully, I didn't enter on the mini-pump that took place on the day of addition, but I still didn't get as good an entry as I could have. I'll blame it on being rusty. Price moved away to the downside from my entry, but I found myself to be much more relaxed about the trades in general than I was in 2014. I guess a lot of this was because I knew that, worst-case scenario, I would lose my entire investment of £400 – an amount I could make back in a few weeks at a part-time job. Sure, the money was from an overdraft, but it was 0% interest in a student account, and the modesty of the amount allowed me to feel no stress about the portfolio at the time.

The one thing I will stress in any conversation with people new to the space, and in this book, is **always** begin with an amount that you aren't scared to lose. That could be £100 or £10,000, depending upon your individual financial situation. Just make your entire trading life much easier and more relaxed by not throwing in the money you require to feed your family, or by taking out a high-interest bank-loan. Sure, you might come out fortunate enough to turn a profit on that critical amount, but considering that the first three to six months of one's trading journey is undoubtedly going to be riddled with losses, don't put yourself in the position of losing money that will bring your world tumbling down. Rant over. Back to the Golem trade.

So, my entry was around 2400 satoshis, and within a few days we were trading maybe 20% below that. Since I was simultaneously working on my dissertation, I knew that day-trading or any form of active trading wasn't going to be the right choice for me, so I made the decision to only play intramonth trades or make cyclical investments, at least until I finished university. I think my Golem position was roughly 30% of my portfolio (high risk allocation is fine in my book when you start out with a very small amount that you can afford to lose). This left me 70% to find a couple more trades, monitor price, shitpost on Twitter, write my dissertation and wait whilst the market cycle unfolded.

A coin whose chart is forever ingrained in my mind as a work of technical artistry is LibraryCredits. If you've been living under the proverbial rock and somehow missed its omnipresence on crypto-Twitter, close this book, load up your favourite charting platform and behold the beauty. However, back in February, this coin had rather little chart history, but the project itself was focused on building a decentralised video-sharing platform, akin to YouTube, and that was something I liked the sound of. From an analytical standpoint, I also loved the range that it was bound within, having completed a near-full retrace of what now was evidently a test-pump. Price had been lingering within the mid-1k satoshi zone for a while, and I was seeing next to nothing about the coin on my Twitter feed. This seemed an opportune entry, and so it was. I picked up a decent chunk in early March at 1500 satoshis, then a little more at 1600 satoshis, and a little more still at 1800 satoshis.

There was one more chart that looked very promising to me, one that I mapped out most extensively: Siacoin. It had completed a bull cycle in the summer of 2016, and the date range from the beginning of the cycle to its peak, and from the peak to the lows in early 2017, were pretty much identical. I love this kind of setup. Price had retraced into a range between mid-20 to mid-30 satoshis, and remained within that area for around twelve weeks, which, from observations on the rest of the markets on Poloniex, was comparatively extensive. The fundamentals behind this coin were also stellar; decentralised storage was something that was in its foundational development back in late 2014/early 2015 but the Sia project seemed to be at the forefront now. It was honestly quite strange picking trades that were so much more ambitious and interesting, fundamentally, than the trades I would take out back then. I had always valued TA above FA, but seeing the new development that was taking place in the space made the fundamental analysis frankly far less dull. I think Siacoin may also have been the first coin I made a public call on since returning, expecting it to make a new all-time high by the end of its next bull cycle, which I had marked out as sometime in late May. I bought in at a 30-satoshi average, and, as far as I can remember, that position, alongside Golem and LibraryCredits, comprised almost my entire portfolio. Now the waiting game began, and, with my positions all set up, I went back to work on the dissertation.

One other thing I had noticed from analysing a number of charts was that market cycles (or pump-and-dumps) had dramatically lengthened in time, with many coins taking two to three months to go from the lows to the peak, unlike the fortnightly (or even weekly) market cycles we had in 2014. Instead, most coins were now pumped like the Darkcoin pump, and this was no doubt partly due to the massive increase in volume that the two years I was away had brought to the space. It was because of this that I did not expect much movement in my trades for at least a couple of weeks, and my attention was split between crypto-Twitter and my work.

As March drew to its end, subtle movements in price had begun, but my focus remained on university. I was getting close to completing my degree, and with that knowledge came an excitement I did not expect for the freedom to focus on crypto. And don't get me wrong, I always preferred alts to forex or other traditional markets, but trading was never a fervent passion of mine, but for some reason the excitement (perhaps expectant of opportunity) was there this time around. The entire altcoin market began to really break out as April arrived, and Bitcoin was now trading 40% above where I bought in – the gains in my positions were being compounded by gains in the fiat value of the mighty 'corn, contrary to 2014. The sheer volume of green markets brought with it a sense of nostalgia: LBC was up above 5000 satoshis, Golem was around 6400 satoshis and Sia was sitting comfortably at 70 satoshis. The gains were strong, and I dumped my Golem if only to secure a first profitable trade. There is something about making a profitable trade that can either destroy you as a trader or fuel you. I say 'destroy' because the unmistakable emotional response following a win can become addictive, and swiftly a trading plan or strategy can be thrown out in search of more of that feeling – this is how one ends up buying tops. However, contrary to the conventional wisdom (which is equally useful) that a trade should be emotionless, from entry to exit, those who have a firm grasp of their emotional responses can utilise the surge of positivity one feels following a win to influence activity levels: for example, after a profitable trade, you will likely feel more spirited and perhaps more enthused. Use that as fuel to research your next trade more meticulously or to analyse a group of charts more sharply etc. It sounds silly, in a way, but it works, and it is something I do every time I close a profitable trade.

The real altcoin bull market began as Bitcoin was breaking through $2000, around mid-May, and my university experience had come to its conclusion. The now-free days were immediately put into the cryptosphere. I began a spreadsheet and journal for coin research, spending around thirty hours poring over Bitcointalk threads, drawing up charts and generally analysing alts to find the most promising trades. My LBC and SC positions were still open, and I had flipped a couple of coins for 200-300% using the profits from the Golem trade in the meantime, but my approach has always been to find new and promising altcoins that are at cyclical lows and push partial profits from open trades into them; rinse and repeat. This is where what has now become my 'research weekend' first came into play and proved its usefulness.

I had branched out to Cryptopia by this point, since many of the coins in my research journal traded primarily on there or on Coinexchange, and the number of altcoins that had incredibly promising charts was a little overwhelming... so many alts, so little spare bitcoin; the shitcoin speculator's perpetual problem. As May turned to June, the gains began to accelerate exponentially, and LBC cracked my primary exit target of 13000 satoshis.

Meanwhile, Siacoin had mapped out price-action almost identically to that which I had predicted for it back in March, and I was able to exit my entire position above 400 satoshis. All that this meant for me was that I could buy a tonne more altcoins. This, ultimately, led to my greatest win in percentage-terms and my first 100x call since returning – Neutron.

As is evident from my Twitter bio, I am now an advisor for the Neutron project, however, back in the summer of 2017, I happened across it whilst looking for coins with the most growth potential on Cryptopia. I had vetted the fundamentals and was keen on them, and the chart was beautiful, with Neutron dumped down below 200 satoshis, having previously been as high as 1700 satoshis, with its market cap being minute. The coin had no premine or ICO (just the way I like it) and the distribution tab on Cryptopia indicated continual accumulation. Back then, the coin was primarily focused on 'simple staking' and its stable masternode network, and I was lucky enough to pick up a fairly large position at around 150 satoshis. I remember tweeting about it at this price-level, suggesting that a 10x was likely given the market conditions and the tiny market cap. A few of you bought. Congratulations.

Within a couple of weeks we had broken back above 1000 satoshis, but the lack of volume and the lack of distribution from the top addresses suggested that this was a shakeout pump, or test pump. I held my entire position and watched price move all the way back to the mid-200 satoshi area. Most would have sat in despair and sold off their position, having thought they had now held through the peak, but I followed my plan and relied on my analysis, and this did not seem like the real move.

Weeks passed by, and still I sat on my position, playing many other shorter-term trades in the meantime, and then it happened, and it happened in a manner utterly reminiscent of 2014; explosively. The second week of July brought with it a slow climb up above 600 satoshis, and price once again popped up into the mid-1000 satoshi range before being slapped down. For the retail-minded, it would look as though we had formed some sort of triple-top below 2000 satoshis, but the mammoth rewards of the long hold soon came through. July 13th saw the triple-top popped, and within hours we had peaked out at nearly 19000 satoshis. 1 9 0 0 0. That's over 12000% from my entry. If that isn't the prime example for why the so-called hodl is supreme, I don't know what is. All of my sell orders were filled, and overall my position returned just under 50x. The spring and summer of 2017 offered a multitude of opportunities just like this, if not greater, and rather than retell each of these, for the sake of brevity it will suffice to say that it was a very good year. Until I got hacked...

Chapter Six

GETTING HACKED

October 2017:

So, following almost eight months of consecutive wins, profitable trading and so on and so forth, something rather devastating happened. To give some context, it was the evening of October 10th, and I had just finished checking up on the laptop I used for local wallet storage and staking. Over the prior couple of months, I had gotten into speculative mining, which is simply the mining of new coins whilst difficulty is very low in expectation of future profits from the growth of the coin. In order to do this, one must have somewhere to mine the coins to, and, since these coins are new, they often had no exchange listings and brand-new, untested wallets. Thus, I had downloaded several new wallets to mine into, and I had been utilising the Bitcointalk forum and a couple of lesser-known forums for announcements, so as to jump on the mining pools as quickly as possible. Here lay one of my primary mistakes – the pursuit of speculative plays to the point at which I was browsing scammy forums for the most profitable coins.

In particular, I was looking for masternode coins with high rewards, and a coin I came across during my search was one called PhantomX, on the Bitcoingarden forum. I downloaded the wallet that I found on the thread, thinking that I had found a potential 100x play (seeing as I was one of the very first people in the mining pool). I pointed my rented rig at the pool, using an address I got from the wallet I'd downloaded, and left it be. Coins came in periodically, and I thought all was going well. After all, my security had flagged up nothing, and the pool was paying out as expected. I went to sleep the night of the 10th and woke up to a nightmare.

My routine then was to check up on the wallets once in the evening and once when I woke up, except this time I found that my CoinonatX wallet, on which I was running a number of masternodes, was empty. Though surprised, at first I thought it was a bug or a glitch, and that, if I relaunched the wallet, I would see my coins again. I closed down the wallet and relaunched to find an empty wallet once again. I clicked on the transactions tab and the entire amount had been withdrawn overnight to an address unknown to me. I began to panic as I realised what had happened. Swiftly, I flicked through all of my various wallets, and each and every one of them was empty, with transactions out at roughly the same time overnight. If I'm honest, I can't recall exactly what I felt in that moment. All I remember is feeling a little shaky and sick, no doubt in a state of shock. **All** of my local storage had been taken. I began panic-tweeting the entire situation as it unfolded, as many of you will remember, trying to deduce how this had happened. I thought to check my exchange wallets, and that's when a bad situation was made even worse. I opened up my Bittrex account to find that the hacker had somehow managed to empty out my balances on there; an exchange I knew to be about as secure as it gets. The sick feeling in my gut grew, and I didn't have a clue what to do. Two-thirds of my altcoin portfolio was gone.

My primary concern was finding out how this had happened, and how only Bittrex had been fleeced but the other exchanges hadn't. My second thought, in truth, was simply relief that I still had something to rebuild from, unlike many who experience this sort of hack. As gut-wrenching as it was, I was fortunate enough to know that: A. altcoin markets are extremely forgiving and B. I still possessed the skill-set that brought me the wealth in the first place. If anything, this was potentially a major setback in a long-term plan, but by no means the end of the journey. Not once did I think that I was going to stop speculating, despite the misery I felt at that time.

After explaining the situation to friends in the space and panic-tweeting it all out, I managed to find out that a Remote Access Trojan in the PhantomX wallet had failed to be picked up by my security software, and it had installed something called TeamViewer onto my PC. I had to Google what that was, but it turns out it's just a piece of software that allows a PC to be controlled remotely. Long story short, my PC was now out of my control, and the hacker was able to use it overnight to fleece my local wallets. Though it made me feel intensely vulnerable and a little bit like I was being watched, at least that made sense. But how had my Bittrex account, of all exchanges, been hacked into? After all, I had enabled 2FA on it, and used U2F keys for my Gmail accounts, and there was no sign of forced entry into those.

Then, as I was cleaning out my PC – deleting wallets and the like prior to a full wipe of my system – I found a screenshot I had taken of my 2FA backup code for

Bittrex... absolute rookie mistake. I have never before done this, and, thinking about it now, I must have just screen-shotted it before copying it down on paper and forgotten to delete the file. An extremely costly mistake, and one that made a bad situation far worse. I set about restoring and reinforcing everything: a full wipe and clean install on my PC; consolidating what remained of my altcoin portfolio; changing passwords; installing new, more robust security software; resetting 2FA and reading and absorbing as much information as I could from the web and from friends alike about all the extra security measures I could have taken.

For example, I learnt about sandboxing and virtual machines for running previously untested or potentially problematic wallets. I also learnt to turn off remote access (which is enabled by default, it seems). Truth be told, I took many steps with regards to my security, but the measures that I didn't have in place at the time were precisely the ones that allowed for a RAT to gain control of my PC, and once that happened and one is unaware of it, there's little else you can do. And whilst, as I have mentioned, I felt utterly devastated about how much hard work was now for nothing and how much of a step back I may have just taken in my long-term plan, my mother reminded me that better it happen at *that* time so that I could learn from it and still have an opportunity to rebuild than happen in the future. It was a painful experience, but a useful lesson nonetheless.

There is always more to know about security, always more you can do, and, in a space like ours, which intrinsically contains more of a cyber-security risk, it must be taken as seriously as any other aspect of your trading, if not more so. Anyway, the hack happened, and I had lost a significant amount of money and a significant portion of my tradeable funds. I was, thankfully, fortunate and smart enough to have prioritised diversification from the outset, and so, my altcoin portfolio did not comprise my entire wealth. Nevertheless, the blow was deep, and I figured it would take me at least twelve months to trade what remained back up to the portfolio value prior to the hack.

I knew that before I could even consider reconvening my trading, I needed to take a break and reset, as I was, of course, emotionally-charged, and those who suffer extreme losses through any means are always the ones who attempt to immediately revenge-trade their way back. This would have been disastrous, and a fortnight of writing this book and occupying my mind with real-life interests and family was in order. What came next was without doubt more overwhelming than the hack itself.

Having rage-tweeted for hours, perhaps inexplicably, I was inundated with support to a degree that I 1. cannot fathom to this day, and 2. could not feasibly keep up with at the time. Over the course of twenty-four hours, I received over a thousand private messages from individuals expressing their support for me, many of whom seemed to feel genuinely upset that this had happened. Honestly, it was more overwhelming than the hack, and those messages kept my spirits from sinking and reinforced the determination I had to come back a fortnight later refreshed and ready to succeed beyond my pre-hack successes. If that wasn't enough, several closer friends in the cryptosphere suggested I create a BTC address for them to donate to and assist in me recouping my losses. I did this, not expecting anything at all outside of what those friends had told me they would donate, and instead received close to 4BTC of donations from a great number of people.

There are few times in life when one is rendered genuinely speechless. This was one. I tried to express the situation to my family and most likely failed to speak comprehensibly, though those hours are a blur. The donations alone recovered a fair portion of my losses, but, more than that, allowed me the capacity to trade myself back to that level without requiring the liquidation of the diversifications that I had set aside for the future. It was an utterly surreal forty-eight hours. Furthermore, I received a message from someone working at Cryptopia, telling me that they had seen the situation unfold on Twitter and managed to track down one of my lost coins (EQT) to an address on the exchange. The individual informed me that I'd need to email them with as much information as I could, but that the withdrawal address from my local wallet matched the deposit address on Cryptopia, and that, though the EQT had been sold already, and some of the resultant bitcoin withdrawn from the exchange, they had managed to freeze what remained, and, given the thumbs-up from their legal team, would be able to return that bitcoin to me. Fast-forward a month, and that chunk of bitcoin was sitting in my Cryptopia account, so I'd like to extend a massive thank you to them for being so helpful and supportive during that time. I had never expected to recover any of my hacked losses outside of my own profitable speculation.

The journey to rebuild my altcoin portfolio had begun in an unexpectedly generous manner, and I felt that the road to a portfolio all-time high was significantly shortened by it. As I mentioned earlier, cryptocurrencies are the most forgiving market of all, and even deep, painful losses can be recovered relatively quickly, and by the end of 2017, I had surpassed these heights. It took less than ten weeks to make a new portfolio all-time high after the hack, and that would undoubtedly have been impossible were it not for the generosity and support of the cryptosphere. Many arrive in the space with their heads filled with the ambition and desire for life-changing financial opportunity, and most stay because they meet genuinely kind and considerate individuals that swiftly become friends. It is the only financial domain that remains fuelled by its charitable roots and compassionate residents. Thank you.

PART TWO: A MANUAL

Chapter One

GETTING STARTED

<u>An Introduction</u>

I sincerely hope that you have enjoyed the read thus far (though I'm sure many may have skipped over the memoir to get straight to this section, and understandably so), and whilst the aims of that material were primarily to amuse and entertain, I have a very different goal for the following chapters. This market is truly one-of-a-kind in its capacity for life-changing opportunities, and, to that end, I would like to provide as much insight as I can to assist in your ability to seize these with both hands. I will seek to explain and elaborate on all possible aspects of the speculative process, specific to altcoins, sharing everything that I have learnt over the past five years in more depth than I have elsewhere.

Now, whilst I will outline many concepts prior to writing in depth, what I shall not do is provide any kind of introduction to trading or cryptocurrencies themselves. This is not an introductory book, and there are plenty available that offer a foundational knowledge of these topics. I would suggest Dominic Frisby's *Bitcoin: The Future of Money?* for a newbie to the cryptosphere, or *Trading in the Zone* by Mark Douglas or any of Alexander Elder's works for those brand-new to trading in general. The following chapters rest on the presupposition that you have a general, foundational understanding of what altcoins are, and of their surrounding infrastructure, alongside a basic knowledge of what trading is, what it comprises of, and the general terminology used, for example, terms such as: price; long; short; patterns; technical analysis; fundamental analysis etc. If these terms are gibberish to you, I have provided a *Key Terminology* section with basic definitions, but, as I've said, we won't be unpacking the very basics in the following chapters.

The reason for this is simply for the sake of brevity: there is plenty of foundational material already available publicly, online and in print, and this book would be twice the length if it was included. What there is a distinct lack of is exhaustive material on altcoin speculation. As such, my aim here is to teach you the process by which I have traded altcoins successfully, as concisely as I can. On the following pages, I have provided a list of all of the tools and platforms that I utilise and may reference at various stages. It is an extensive list, comprising of a number of exchanges, statistics compilers, coin filters, charting platforms and anything else one could possibly require the use of. Alongside each, I have given a brief description of their utility.

Key Resources

Exchanges:

Bittrex: https://bittrex.com/ - My primary altcoin trading exchange. A top-ten exchange by volume. Reliable and integral to the cryptosphere. Strong security features.

Binance: https://www.binance.com/ - A relatively new exchange that has taken the number one spot for volume. New listings are particularly of interest as they tend to experience explosive growth once listed due to the enormous volume available.

Poloniex: https://poloniex.com/ - Particularly useful for orderbook analysis.

Cryptopia: https://www.cryptopia.co.nz/ - My favourite exchange, primarily because of the immense opportunity for rapid portfolio growth. It lists most of the larger, more established coins, but, most significantly, hundreds of newer, smaller altcoins, which may possess greater upside potential than coins on other exchanges. Also offer a variety of security features.

CoinExchange: https://www.coinexchange.io/ - Another exchange I rarely use but one that is solely utilised for microcap plays. New coins tend to be listed here before the larger exchanges, so it is useful when looking for early accumulation opportunities.

BitMEX: https://www.bitmex.com/ - An exchange offering margin trading on a number of cryptocurrencies.

Statistics/Data:

Coinmarketcap: https://coinmarketcap.com/ - The primary resource for researching altcoin statistics.

CoinGecko: https://www.coingecko.com/en – Another great resource for statistics and data, with much overlap with Coinmarketcap. Offers extra, in-built features, such as basic overviews, mining calculators and on-site discussion forums.

BitScreener: https://bitscreener.com/ - Useful for further chart analysis than the previous two websites. Also provides recent related news.

AtomSignal: https://atomsignal.com – Provides useful data on altcoin markets from the larger exchanges, including the tracking of buy and sell 'walls'.

WenMoon: http://wenmoon.com – Great, simple website for more in-depth filtering of coins than is possible on Coinmarketcap. Useful during the research process.

BitcoinTalk: https://bitcointalk.org/ - The home of new altcoin announcement threads, general discussion etc. I use it primarily for fundamental analysis.

Charting:

Coinigy: https://www.coinigy.com/ - Incorporates the TradingView platform but for a greater number of cryptocurrency exchanges. My principal charting platform.

TradingView: https://uk.tradingview.com/ - The world's charting platform. Offers free charting of all traditional markets, as well as cryptocurrencies from the largest exchanges.

BitcoinWisdom: https://bitcoinwisdom.com/ - I monitor Bitcoin's price using this website. Very clean and user-friendly. Fewer features makes it uncluttered.

Portfolio Tracker:

Blockfolio – The original app for portfolio tracking.
Delta – An alternative to Blockfolio, and one that I have come to use more often.

Miscellaneous:

ICT: https://www.youtube.com/user/InnerCircleTrader – Much of the price-action analysis that I incorporate in my trading was learned through material by ICT. I suggest finding whatever tutorials you can by him and studying them intensively.

Key Terminology

- **Accumulation**: The process by which one builds a position in a coin.
- **Arbitrage**: The differing prices between exchanges for the same market.
- **Ask/Bid**: Sell orders (ask) and buy orders (bid) in the orderbook on an exchange.
- **Averaging Down**: The process of lowering the average entry cost of one's position by buying lower incrementally.
- **Bag**: A position in a coin.
- **Bagholder**: Someone who possesses an underwater position in a coin.
- **Bots**: Automated trading on exchanges.
- **Bull/Bear**: The expectation of higher (bull) or lower (bear) prices.
- **Circulating Supply/Total Supply/Maximum Supply**: The amount of a coin currently available for transactions (circulating supply); the amount of a coin currently in existence (total supply); the maximum amount of a coin that can ever come into existence (maximum supply).
- **Cryptocurrencies/Cryptoassets/Altcoins/ Coins**: Though there are definitional differences, for the purposes of the following chapters, these terms will be used interchangeably to denote any tradeable digital market.
- **Distribution**: The process by which one reduces one's position in a coin.
- **FOMO**: Fear of missing out.

- **Fractal**: A pattern of price-action that is observed to be repeating (or have repeated) on any scale.
- **FUD**: Fear, uncertainty and doubt.
- **Fundamental Analysis**: The evaluation of a coin based on its intrinsic properties, its prospects, its utility and its community, as well as macro factors, such as the economic and sectoral landscape.
- **HODL**: Originally, this was a mistype by a drunk individual on the Bitcointalk forum, but has recently come to be adopted as 'Hold On for Dear Life', after comments by the CFTC Chairman, Chris Giancarlo.
- **Intraday/Intraweek/Intramonth/Position**: Trades that are intended to be entered and exited within a day/a week/a month/over a month.
- **Leverage**: The ability to borrow capital against your initial position in order to magnify your exposure.
- **Limit Order**: An order that is set to be executed when price hits the level predefined in the order itself.
- **Liquidity**: The ability to buy or sell a coin without moving price. Illiquid markets suffer from greater volatility.
- **Margin Trading**: The use of leverage to open a position greater than your level of capital.
- **Market Cap**: The market capitalisation of a coin can be calculated either by multiplying the price of the coin by its circulating supply (to find its current market cap – also defined as 'network value') or by its maximum supply (to find the maximum network

value when all coins have come into existence). For the purpose of this book, I will be using the former calculation, unless specified.

- **Market-Maker**: For the purposes of this book, this is the orchestrator of the major movements in price in a market.
- **Market Order**: An order to buy or sell at the current price level, executed immediately.
- **Masternode**: The collateral used as a means of securing a coin's network, which provides rewards for the owner periodically as long as the masternode is live.
- **Microcap/Lowcap/Midcap/Highcap**: A microcap is a coin with a market cap between 0-25BTC; lowcap, 25-250BTC; midcap, 250-2500BTC; and a highcap has a market cap above 2500BTC.
- **OHLC**: The four values depicted by a candlestick on a chart – the open, high, low and close.
- **Order Depth**: A chart found on exchanges that illustrates the amount of buy orders vs sell orders in the market.
- **OTC**: Over-the-counter, or non exchange-based, trades.
- **Pattern**: A predictive price formation.
- **Premine**: The amount of a coin that was mined in the genesis block, usually for the purposes of development.
- **Pump-and-dump**: The artificial engineering of explosive upwards movement that is followed by even more explosive selling. In crypto, almost every market cycle of every altcoin is a heavily-

manipulated pump-and-dump, rather than fundamentally-based growth.

- **Rich-List**: The list of addresses found on a coin's block explorer that depicts the largest holders of that coin and their transactions.
- **Risk**: Either, the percentage of your portfolio occupied by a position, or, the level of volatility in the market for any given coin.
- **ROI**: Return-on-investment.
- **Stop-Loss**: An order that is set to be executed if price trades below the predefined level, in an attempt to prevent further losses.
- **Support/Resistance**: Price-levels that have historically been reliable points at which market participants have heavily bought (support) or sold (resistance).
- **Technical Analysis**: The method of evaluation that is entirely dependent upon a coin's chart, with the chart being an illustration of that coin's price-history.
- **Walls**: Extremely large orders in the orderbook.
- **Whale**: A market participant with a sizeable position, far greater than the average individual.
- **Volume**: The amount of any given coin traded across a predefined time-period.

Chapter Two
FUNDAMENTAL ANALYSIS

Fundamental analysis can seem a complex process for anybody new to the cryptosphere. With thousands of altcoins in existence – each of which may be built on one or more of the many algorithms currently utilised, and which may operate using a number of different reward and verification systems (PoW, PoS etc.) – the space undoubtedly feels daunting to evaluate. There are so many subtleties to each individual coin – so many variables – and a mass of tools available for analysis due to the decentralised nature of the technology. Though, at first, this may seem somewhat of a barrier to entry, it is actually a gift. The process is time-consuming, for sure, but in what other markets is there such transparency to be exploited? Though neglecting fundamental analysis in the preliminary stages of my journey as a trader, it has become an indispensable tool that I use hand-in-hand with technical analysis, particularly when entering a new position. The one caveat to this is that, unlike technical analysis, I never base a trade entirely on its fundamentals. There have been many occasions (and without doubt shall be many more) where I have entered a trade simply because I found the chart too delicious to pass up despite poor fundamentals. This has never happened in reverse. If I'm not keen on a chart, I will discard that coin until the chart becomes appealing, regardless of where my fundamental analysis of it lies. That being said, where I think FA trumps its technical counterpart is in imagination; one can discover in the fundamentals the potential of a coin beyond what its chart may suggest, and, when a trade enters uncharted territory, FA can be critical in finding an exit.

This chapter will be broken down into following sectors of analysis:

Coins: The intrinsic properties of the coin, such as its block reward, coin supply, premine etc.

Exchanges: How I use exchange listings to assess price potential.

Block Explorers and Rich-Lists: One of the primary forms of fundamental analysis I use when evaluating a coin. I will dig into how to spot accumulation and smart-money, as well as how to use this information for exits.

Community: Social media presence, marketing, community spirit and loyalty, and responsiveness and approachability, and how these each affect price.

Development: Roadmaps, whitepapers, websites, wallets, protocols, masternodes etc. The bulk of where a coin's fundamental potential lies.

These five pillars of fundamental analysis will make up everything that you should require in order to form an opinion on the intrinsic potential of any given coin. The potential (or scope for growth) is the most important thing to consider when evaluating a coin fundamentally, at least for our purposes of generating a profit on our positions. The fundamental analysis one would take out if the goal was to find the most suitable coin for anonymity or the most stable network for storing one's wealth would be entirely different. The approach I adopt is strictly for a speculator. Simply put, the higher the growth potential of the coin, the more likely I am to allocate part of my portfolio to it. Anyway, to spare you from further introduction, I will begin with the first aspect of analysis: the coin itself.

Coins

Each coin lies somewhere on the spectrum between absolute shitcoin on one end and revolutionary on the other; though, admittedly, the vast majority belong to the former. Not only do they lie on this spectrum, but they also exist on another, and that is *growth* (or pump) potential, and this is largely centred on the coin's intrinsic properties. Some parameters and specifications actually lend themselves to be more easily manipulated by market-makers for more dynamic (and thus profitable) price movement, and this can be observed by simply looking at the trends in the kinds of coins that grow exponentially. Though there are and always will be anomalies, a coin's internally-coded variables play a huge part in whether it draws the interest of smart-money or not.

Now, some coins, given the aforementioned spectrums, are absolute shitcoins with poor growth potential, and some are the exact opposite. The goal of analysing the coin itself is to enter as few positions that occupy the former end of those spectrums as I possibly can. You will always get a few losers, but I have found this number to have reduced immensely since filtering for the parameters that I shall lay out in this section. Of a coin's many and varied parameters, there are two that have proved critical to how explosively a coin can grow in price, generally-speaking, and these are *coin supply* and *block structure* (reward and time). Additionally, the existence of a premine is something that is important to consider.

Coin Supply: Coin supply is a parameter that has numerous effects on growth potential. Not only this, but there are actually three categories of coin supply: circulating; total; and maximum. I will go through each of these categories in depth, assessing how changes in these figures would influence a coin's growth, and how they influence my decisions.

Circulating Supply: First up is circulating supply, which I consider the most significant parameter of the three. The reason for this is simply because circulating supply affects your trade directly, unlike the other two parameters. Coins at the two extremes of the following spectrum should be discarded immediately: circulating supplies below six digits or above multi-billions are not conducive to firm control of price by a market-maker, and thus are likely to be neglected by smart-money. Also, coins with truly low circulating supplies (I've seen alts with as few as forty-two coins in existence) tend to be ones created for novelty purposes, or for the amusement of their developer. The primary reason why I ignore the two extremes is because of their effect on the orderbooks, and a negative effect on the orderbook makes a coin ultimately more difficult to profit from. To clarify, if a coin has a circulating supply in the billions, the likelihood is that the orderbook will be extremely congested at the lower satoshi values.

Take Mooncoin, for example. MOON has a circulating supply of 223bn coins at the time of writing this, and a market cap of around 4400BTC ($38mn), with average trading volume for the day sitting at just over 1BTC. The

lower end of the orderbook for Mooncoin on CoinExchange
reads as follows:

Buy Orders:

Price	MOON	BTC
0.00000001BTC	384217412.41346593	38.44217412

Sell Orders:

Price	MOON	BTC
0.00000002BTC	118848573.22407949	2.37697146
0.00000003BTC	718824773.28290095	21.56474320
0.00000004BTC	520742185.98276171	20.82968744
0.00000005BTC	400691388.03185507	20.03456940
0.00000006BTC	390916162.85328233	23.45496877

Now, look at that and tell me that looks appealing. The
issue with these sorts of coins is that they require
significantly more Bitcoin to move them. The example I
have given depicts 87BTC of sell orders to move the coin a
few hundred percent. Whilst one might quite rightly argue
that that is a remarkable move, it is saddled with many
negatives that do not exist for coins with lower circulating
supplies than this: firstly, there is the distinct possibility
that a coin like this could actually fall through its buy
support at 1 satoshi, especially if some large orders begin
being dumped into it. Weak hands could then crumble this
market, as the psychological factors push them to the
thought that they need to exit before others otherwise risk
not having any way to exit at all. This is an unnecessary
stress to give yourself, given the abundance of tradeable
alts. Plus, the opposite phenomenon appears in coins with
lower supplies, as their prices naturally trade at higher

denominations, and thus, if (or when) price trades down a digit, say from 1000 satoshis to 950 satoshis, this seems a bargain, in the same way that £10 for a product always sounds a little too much but £9.99 feels a steal. Secondly, this particular coin, as I have mentioned, has a 24-hour trading volume of around 1BTC. Given that it would require 87BTC of buying to move it to 6 satoshis, the increase in volume necessary to facilitate such a move would be even greater. Thirdly, the orderbook itself becomes infinitely more difficult to read, and thus more difficult to analyse and exploit – a tool that is indispensable when trading altcoins, and that I will go into in its own section later in the book. Unlike altcoins with low to mid-level circulating supplies – and by that, the range I'm describing is generally between 1 million to 1 billion coins – the coins that have these far larger circulating supplies occupy the lowest end of the orderbook, and thus, orders are often amalgamated, making it near-impossible to identify patterns that would be insightful. The market-maker's orders become indistinguishable from the rest of the orders, as can be seen from the Mooncoin example.

Do not put your options for meticulous analysis (and therefore success) at an immediate disadvantage by picking coins with extremely high circulating supplies, despite the obvious fact that one could profit from them if one picked correctly. There are far too many opportunities for success in this space for you to concern yourself with those that are more challenging. There are those that would argue that an exceedingly large supply naturally gives the individual coin a greatly diminished dollar value, relative to other altcoins, and thus this would provide psychological reasoning for entering a position, in expectation that new market participants would flock to these coins with the perception that a low dollar value implies cheapness. Whilst this can be true, and has been demonstrated by recent pumps of low-satoshi coins, this is, in effect, gambling. There is no analysis taking place here, fundamental or otherwise – it is merely a bet on the stupidity of new traders. Again, there are far too many opportunities in the space for one to just take a punt like this. And, the same applies for minimal circulating supplies – anything below six digits is a no-go, unless there is a legitimate fundamental reason for the supply being so low. An example of legitimacy would be Primalbase Token, which has a circulating supply fixed at 1,000 tokens, each of which can be bought and held to be used as a 'key' with which one can book out office space in real-world locations. It makes sense for PBT to limit their supply of tokens to such a low figure, given the limitations of workspace availability in each location. However, this is an anomaly, as most altcoins with such a low circulating supply are merely so for the sake of novelty.

Now that we can use the circulating supply to filter our altcoin picks within a certain range (I repeat, the range I use is generally 1mn to 1bn coins), I will elaborate on how this range is most useful for successful trades. Let us take Blackcoin (BLK) as an example. Blackcoin has a circulating supply of 76.6mn coins, and a market cap of 2931BTC ($28.1mn) at the time of writing this. A coin with a circulating supply of this amount is far more useful for a market-maker, and thus, for the growth potential of the coin, than our Mooncoin example. This is predominantly because of the freedom that such a circulating supply offers within the orderbook for the Blackcoin market, hence allowing for greater control of price by the whales. Greater control of price lends itself to a better orchestrated bull cycle and the capacity for extensive growth, since the market-maker can effectively accumulate and distribute by exploiting the space within the orderbook – a technique we will dive into later. The point is that it is coins within this range of circulating supply that are perfect for full control of price-action, therefore it is these coins that you need to filter for. Following the smart-money is how you continually win.

Let's look at a portion of the Blackcoin orderbook, if only to illuminate the vast differences between it and the MOON orderbook:

Buy Orders:

Price	BLK	BTC
0.00003817	22248.08816964	0.8492
0.00003760	271.47227793	0.0102
0.00003751	210.39086397	0.0079
0.00003750	500.00000000	0.0187
0.00003737	2600.36963305	0.0971
0.00003736	12230.0000000	0.4569

Sell Orders:

Price	BLK	BTC
0.00003820	4138.48153065	0.1581
0.00003823	920.62505299	0.0352
0.00003871	52.11631318	0.0020
0.00003900	350.00000000	0.0137
0.00003941	1968.00000000	0.0776

It is quite evident just on first glance that the orderbook for BLK provides much more breathing space for orders, and the larger orders can at once be distinguished from the smaller ones. This will be critical in the following chapters, and will provide you with the opportunity to analyse all manner of significant information, such as when might be a good entry or exit, what the market-maker is intending to do with price in the short or long term, and whether accumulation is taking place, all of which cannot be accurately evaluated in coins with far larger circulating supplies.

The caveat to all of this (and where the anomalies will be found) is that there is some dependency on market capitalisation that must be taken into account. The two parameters go hand-in-hand when researching for a new position, and though I will go into more depth on market caps in another section, I will briefly explain why these two subjects of analysis must be considered together: market caps are correlated with circulating supplies when it comes to our primary evaluation; the congestion of the orderbook. An altcoin with a circulating supply in the billions can be accommodated by a very high market cap, as is the case with Ripple (XRP), which has a circulating supply of 39bn coins, but due to its immense 4.5mn BTC market cap ($43.6bn), its orderbook is very liquid, uncongested and is not restricted to the single-digit satoshi region. Thus, it is less impractical to analyse for market manipulation. A mammoth market cap is what is required for a coin of abnormally high circulating supply to become tradeable, but this is actually another reason why I stay away from such alts, as the aim of speculation is maximal growth – growth that cannot be achieved by having positions in coins that are already trading at a market cap in the billions of dollars. Stick to the range, and you will find the most optimal opportunities, even if you miss a few winners.

Total Supply: The second supply parameter of significance is total supply. This can be defined as the total amount of any given cryptocurrency in existence, and is usually calculated by adding the circulating supply to the amount of that coin that has been created but that is not in circulation. For example, the circulating supply of Linx (LINX) is currently 17.4mn, but its total supply is 18.4mn. The 1mn difference between these figures is simply due to the 1% premine of the maximum supply of 100mn coins. This premine is not included in Coinmarketcap's calculations for circulating supply, since premined coins are generally locked up for a period of time, or are very slowly introduced into circulation when the coins are used to pay for whatever the developers required the premine for.

Total supply is, in my opinion, the least important to consider of the three supply parameters, but this doesn't make it insignificant. It is actually quite a prominent component of my filtering process. Right off the bat, I will discard any coin from my research list that has a total supply to circulating supply ratio greater than 2:1. So, if a coin has a circulating supply of 10 million coins, its total supply should not exceed 20 million. The reason I filter for this is because 50% is the maximum amount of coins out of circulation that I care to accept from an altcoin, and even that is rare − my optimal range is between 0-20% of total coins out of circulation. This, I understand, is purely preferential rather than an objective mode of analysis, but my reasoning is as follows: the more coins there are outside of the circulating supply, the more research (and constant research, at that) one has to do to remain on top of where that supply is. Having 70% of the total supply out of circulation may not seem, to you, a huge problem, but it can become a huge problem if you do not track that supply throughout the course of holding a position in that coin.

Crypto is still very much the Wild West, especially if you are attempting to turn a profit speculating on less established altcoins. Too many times have I seen a large premine or 'developer fund' be neglected by traders, and that uncirculated supply swiftly flood the market when those developers decide that price is high enough for them to take an early retirement. This is why even 50% of the supply being out of circulation, regardless of whether it is 'locked' in development fund addresses, is a risk that I do not often like to take. Sure, these funds can usually be tracked very well, but all it takes is you being away from your trading setup when the discovery is made that the supposedly secured premine has been transferred to an exchange and the orderbook has been flattened to turn you into a 'member of the community', as we like to call those who are left holding the bag with no feasible method of exit. It just isn't worth it.

So, discard the altcoins that seem like a bargain until you find out that two-thirds of the total supply is uncirculated, and whittle down your picks to those that allow you to be as well-informed as possible: namely, the coins that have the vast majority of their total supply in circulation, available to be bought and sold by market participants at will.

There is another reason why this is important to consider, and that is that total supply affects growth potential for what may now seem an obvious reason: what market-maker is going to put a serious amount of capital into a coin for the purposes of pushing up its value if they cannot account for 80% of the supply? And, if they do, they would be incredibly short-sighted to do so, since they would be at the whim of whoever controls the majority of the supply. Their accumulation and distribution could be disrupted, and **they** could be the ones left holding the bag, since they are providing the liquidity for the market, and, as such, a rogue developer or team could use that liquidity to dump their supply. That doesn't sound like smart-money to me. The market-makers for coins with these large discrepancies between circulating supply and total supply tend to be poor, both in capital and in their ability to manipulate price effectively, so steer clear.

Now, I know I have stressed this before, but I will mention it again: I am speaking generally, and of course there will be anomalies, but the aim is to find the most optimal opportunities for profit, and those do not often come from coins with a far greater total supply than their circulating supply.

Maximum Supply: Maximum supply is an important factor in my analysis for one very simple reason: the maximum supply will tell you whether a coin is going to suffer from large levels of inflationary pressure (though block structure plays a part in this, and we'll get to that in the next section) or not. This is a huge component in the growth potential of any given cryptocurrency, and projects that may seem like goldmines can become very costly, longer-than-intended positions if one does not pay attention to maximum supply. I use this parameter in a number of ways, and its use differs depending on whether I am looking at a brand-new coin or one that has been in existence for a while. For example, with a new project, I am wary of the fact that very little of the maximum supply has come into existence, and, as such, its current market cap is deceiving, and thus the value of an entry is obscured. Let's run through an example to illustrate this more clearly:

Take, for instance, Coin X (CX). CX launched a week ago, and has had 100,000 coins come into existence since. It has been listed on an exchange, and is currently trading at 0.0001BTC per CX, giving it a current market cap of 10BTC. You are impressed with the project, and all other aspects of your analysis point to this being a promising coin to buy. At a 10BTC market cap, one would imagine the only way is up for the price of the coin. However, you have neglected to look at the coin's maximum supply, which just so happens to be 1bn coins. A maximum supply of this magnitude would put CX at a **maximum** market cap of 100,000BTC at current prices. That puts its ultimate valuation within the top 30 coins currently in existence. It is obvious to see how significantly this devalues an entry at current prices, as one is essentially betting that demand will continue to grow equal to, or greater than, the growth of the supply. I would not take this entry except in the following circumstance (the caveat I mentioned before): the block reward structure is set up so that the 1bn coins will not come into existence for many, many years, and, as such, the inflation rate, despite this vast difference between circulating supply and maximum supply, is actually rather low. In fact, even in the example given above, if the supply emission remained constant, it would take around twenty-eight years for CX to reach its maximum supply, which gives an entry at 0.0001BTC much more value. If supply emission grew exponentially rather than invariably, and maximum supply would be reached within two to three years, I would hold off on entry until more of the maximum supply has come into existence so that the market can settle at a price that gives us – the speculator – more value.

So, when analysing maximum supply for a coin, I am looking at the ratio between it and the circulating supply. If circulating supply is less than 25% of maximum supply, I know that further research must be done on the *emission* of supply in order to get a better idea of what constitutes a low (and thus, far more likely to be profitable) entry for that coin. In the case of a well-established coin – one that has been in existence for over a year – I am generally of the opinion that the higher the ratio of circulating supply to maximum supply, the greater the chance of me making a successful trade, especially for those of us who are looking at longer-term positions, as a coin's inflation rate has a much larger impact given a greater duration. Ideally, I would like to take an entry in a coin that has over two-thirds of its maximum supply in circulation, as, by that point, inflation as percentage per day is negligible. It is rare to find a coin like this that is also promising fundamentally in its other aspects **and** is trading at its lows on the chart, but those are, of course, the diamonds that I am always looking out for.

Block Structure: Block structure analysis picks up where we left off with maximum supply, in that these two parameters must be assessed in unison rather than separately, since that is how they can be most effectively exploited. By 'block structure', I am referring to the block reward and block time parameters. These two details offer some insight on the growth potential of a coin by providing us with that coin's inflation rate. Using some basic calculations, one can use these parameters to work out roughly what the coin's circulating supply will be at any given moment in the future, and, from this, one can work out the rate of inflation. This is best clarified with an example. Let's look at Dogecoin (DOGE):

DOGE has a clear block reward schedule that reads as follows:

> **Block 1-99,999**: 0-1,000,000 Dogecoin
> **Block 100,000 — 144,999**: 0-500,000 Dogecoin
> **Block 145,000 — 199,999**: 250,000 Dogecoin
> **Block 200,000 — 299,999**: 125,000 Dogecoin
> **Block 300,000 — 399,999**: 62,500 Dogecoin
> **Block 400,000 — 499,999**: 31,250 Dogecoin
> **Block 500,000 — 599,999**: 15,625 Dogecoin
> **Block 600,000+**:10,000 Dogecoin

Given that DOGE has a block time of 60 seconds, the average number of blocks mined per hour is also 60, and 1440 for the day. From the block reward schedule, we can see that the block reward becomes smallest after 600,000 blocks have been mined, which would take around 417 days, or a little over a year. This is a relatively swift progression from high block reward to low block reward, and thus, the supply emission is very high during the earliest stages of the mining schedule. If we rewind to Dogecoin's launch, it would be a poor choice as a speculator to have entered a position during those early stages, as circulating supply was growing rapidly but was low enough to allow for an inflated price. Below is the Dogecoin chart that clearly depicts that those who had bought during the first few months after launch would have bought at a premium, and it would have been much more opportune to have waited for the vast majority of the block-halvings to have occurred.

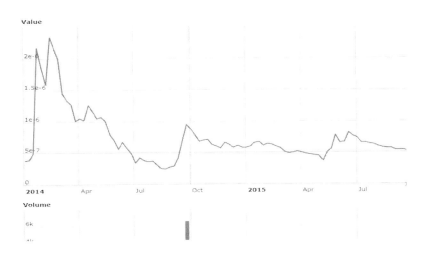

As you can see, anyone who bought prior to August 2014 will have been underwater almost immediately after entry, and anyone who entered prior to May 2014 will have been underwater for over a year. The unlucky individuals who bought between mid-February and March 2014 will **STILL** be underwater, almost four years later. This is simply because they neglected supply emission. In March 2014, Dogecoin was priced above 200 satoshis, primarily because of hype at the time but also because the circulating supply at that time was around 55bn coins. Five months later, circulating supply was 90bn coins – an increase of around 60%. Simply put, there was too much supply coming onto the market to retain that price-level. And that is the potential disaster you can run into if the block structure of a coin is disregarded prior to opening a new position.

So, how exactly do I use the block structure to aid my fundamental analysis? Firstly, I tend not to buy alts that have invariable supply emissions over their entire trajectory – that is, if a coin's circulating supply is predetermined to come into existence at a constant rate, I discard it immediately. The reason for this is because it makes it more difficult to judge a good entry, since the sell pressure on the market from miners or stakers or masternode holders has the potential to be unchanging over time, whereas, in a coin that has a declining rate of supply emission, the sell pressure, by definition, cannot be unchanging; it would decrease as the coin ages, and that is promising for a speculator.

To make this clearer, I often do a calculation that informs me of the maximum sell pressure that an altcoin could face with each new day (and, through this, I can also assess the inflation rate). Imagine Coin A (CA) has a current circulating supply of 1mn coins, and is being mined at a rate of 1440 blocks per day (60-second block times) with a block reward of 50 CA. This would mean that 72,000 CA are coming into existence each day. The current market price of CA is 5000 satoshis (and thus, its circulating market cap is 50BTC). Using the current market price, we can work out that, with 72,000 CA being created daily, there is a maximum sell pressure of 3.6BTC worth of **new** coins per day, which is indicative of the demand required to facilitate that new supply. Furthermore, we can work out the inflation rate from this information: 3.6BTC is 7.2% (3.6/50*100) of the market cap being added with each new day. 7.2% inflation each day (this would incrementally decrease, of course, as circulating supply increases) is huge, and does not make a particularly strong case for current prices to be a valuable entry for a speculator, especially for one looking at a time-frame greater than a month. In general, I am looking for entries on altcoins that have, at most, 2% daily inflation (decreasing incrementally each day). Though, the less inflation, the better.

A coin's inflation rate influences market dynamics in an obvious way, as it makes the manipulation of price significantly more difficult if the market-maker is battling a large amount of supply coming onto the market on a daily basis. Take Zcash (ZEC), for example. Every time that coin looks like it wants to break out, it is pushed back down by the sheer volume of sell pressure that it faces due to its inflation rate. This is a problem that you want to try to avoid where possible, thus giving your trade a greater probability for swifter success – swifter success allows for your capital to be reinvested into the plethora of opportunities in the space, rather than holding onto a position until its supply emission slows down enough to make it feasible for the market-maker to push price upwards.

To summarise, when analysing a coin's block structure, you are looking for the most optimal supply emission or inflation rate. Less than 2% daily inflation is a must when considering newly-launched coins for longer-term positions. Less than 100% annual inflation is ideal for more established coins. And, prior to all entries, do your calculations to figure out how much potential sell pressure could be coming onto the market daily, and how expensive an entry at current prices will end up when projected forward through the block reward schedule.

Premine: Ah, premines; a topic of much contention within the cryptosphere. Some argue that a large premine is, in fact, an advantage for the growth of a coin, as it allows for sufficient resources for developers from the outset to expend on marketing, exchange listings, recruitment, living expenses so that they can devote their entire being to the project, and all manner of other reasoning. Others argue that a premine is the first sign that an alt is just another scam that will be exploited and left to die once the developers fleece the community of just enough liquidity to dump their allocations and run. I happen to lie somewhere in the middle of these two positions, though, admittedly, closer to the latter than the former.

I am of the opinion that a particularly large premine is a giant red flag, and I will once again use the argument of abundance as my reasoning for why such projects are swiftly discarded when I'm looking for a new coin. There are simply far too many alts being created every day (and far too many already in existence) to justify, as a speculator, choosing a coin that has inherently more risk than one without a premine. One reason why I don't subscribe so readily to the argument that a large premine allows for greater development, and thus larger growth, is that the vast majority of these coins being created (that we will undoubtedly be accumulating at some time or other) are doing very little that is new, as, for every clone with a large premine – no matter how visually appealing their branding – there will be a handful that have accomplished or are accomplishing the same goals with little to no premine. So, yes, the premine may provide that particular project with immediate resources with which to progress with their roadmaps and achieve their aims, but there are plenty of alts – and plenty of developers – who have been able to do so without one.

Instead, look for coins that are funded by the team behind the project, or, even more promisingly, endeavouring to grow using the community they build as a driving force for necessary resources for development. By opting for the community-funded route over the far easier route of a premine, the coin is embedding within itself an inextricable value that premined coins may not have; a dedicated user-base who are committed to the growth of the project. And that is fundamentally invaluable. After all, this is still the Wild West, and having witnessed a great number of runaway devs, dumped premines etc. I simply do not feel that one's capital is required to take on that inherent risk in order to profit from the growth of the space. It is better to be safe than sorry, especially as a beginner. The last thing you want is to enter a position in a coin with a large premine, witness the premine being dumped and your position losing the majority of its value, and feel emotionally incapable of progressing on your journey for fear of experiencing that again.

With regards to what I deem an acceptable premine, I have little to no issue with one that totals less than 5%. Anything above that, up to 10%, would have to be seriously justified, and I would have to be very confident in all the other aspects of analysis. Above 10% is just unnecessarily large – if a coin has a premine above 10%, it would need to be a very well-established coin with a public team and an impeccable chart for me to consider entering, but this is a rarity. In general, 0-1% is what I am filtering for. No premine is the best premine.

Market Capitalisation: Another fan favourite in the cryptosphere is the concept of market capitalisation, which is simply the price of a coin multiplied by either, its circulating supply, its total supply or its maximum supply, depending on what the individual is looking for. I tend to almost exclusively be referring to circulating market cap (price multiplied by circulating supply) when I talk about the market cap of a coin. Maximum market cap is useful for the same reason that maximum supply is useful: it allows you to value your position not just at current prices but also at the point at which the coin's entire supply has come into existence. However, for the purposes of this section, we will focus on market cap as calculated using circulating supply, as it provides the most insight on potential growth **and** for assessing potential exits.

Before we get into the gritty details, I think it will be useful for me to outline the four categories of market cap that I use, as this is something I am often asked about. These four categories are microcaps, lowcaps, midcaps and highcaps, and I identify them as follows:

Microcaps: **0-25BTC** (roughly $0-250,000 at current prices)
Lowcaps: **25-250BTC** (roughly $250,000-2.5mn)
Midcaps: **250BTC-2500BTC** (roughly $2.5mn-25mn)
Highcaps: **2500BTC and above** (roughly $25mn+)

I list these categories by bitcoin amount over dollar amount because of the current volatility of the BTC price. Back in January and February 2017, BTC pretty much hovered around $1000, and it made sense to use dollar valuations to differentiate between these categories, but as Bitcoin has grown explosively, these dollar valuations have shifted dramatically and continue to do so every day with Bitcoin's volatility. So, around mid-2017, I found it helpful to categorise alts by their BTC market caps, and I just used anecdotal evidence to guide me with the figures. I recognised that a coin with a market cap of under 25BTC would be incredibly easy for anyone with even a small amount of capital to manipulate, and that the level of capital required for significant price movement increased dramatically when this was raised to 250BTC, and more so at 2500BTC. Thus, I picked these values with which to differentiate between a microcap, a lowcap, a midcap and a highcap. Admittedly, it takes a little getting used to, relative to dollar valuations, but it's far simpler than continually changing the categories based on the Bitcoin price.

Now, this book is unquestionably geared towards microcaps and lowcaps, with some midcap material mingled in. The reason for this, and for my adoration of these two categories over everything else, is because market cap is directly correlated to growth potential. A microcap has an infinitely higher probability of growing 100x over a highcap. Think about an altcoin like Dash. Dash currently has a market cap of 487,204BTC ($4.6bn). There is absolutely no chance that Dash is going to grow 100x from where it currently sits. It is just not feasible. Now consider Neuro (NRO), which has a market cap of 17BTC ($157k). 100x growth on Neuro would take it to 1700BTC ($15.7mn). That would be a midcap.

The growth potential of these smaller, less-established coins is immense, and whilst the majority of them are 100% shitcoins, there are many that are not and that are extremely undervalued relative to similar projects. It is this undervaluation that we are looking to take advantage of. Remember the goal I set out at the beginning of this half of the book: the aim is explosive growth, not minimal growth. If you're looking for a safe and secure 10% annual return, buy some equities and get yourself back in that office – those inventory reports won't analyse themselves. The magic of the cryptosphere is in its unique capacity to turn a very small amount of money into a significant amount of money, and microcaps and lowcaps are where that magic happens. Sure, the highcaps can be very profitable to day-trade when you already have a large amount of capital – certainly more so than day-trading forex or equities – but this book is for those of us who didn't have much capital to begin with. $500 worth of Bitcoin, Ethereum and Dash just cannot give you the same returns as the smaller projects in the space, and, with proper risk management, investing in them **can** be no more risky than the more established alts but with significantly higher upside.

We've discovered that microcaps and lowcap coins are what we want to be searching for during our research, but how can we best utilise these market caps in our speculation? The primary insight garnered from the market cap figure, outside of the obvious point that a smaller project has far more upside potential, is in picking an exit (or several). Whilst I predominantly use technical analysis to set targets and exits for all of my positions, market cap analysis is one way of supplementing these with a fundamental grounding.

For example, Bytecent (BYC) has a market cap of 177BTC ($1.9mn), and so, would fit into our lowcap category. It has a circulating supply of around 2mn; real-world partnerships; its own mining mechanism named Proof-of-Bytecent; a dedicated team of developers and has been in existence since early 2015. Naturally, there is much more to the fundamental analysis of BYC, but we'll stick with the few things I have just mentioned. From this point, I would look for altcoins that are similar in their design and function to BYC. You can do this with a simple Google search of the keywords associated with the coin you are analysing, or by browsing the Bitcointalk threads, or simply asking around on social media if anybody is aware of a similar or copycat project. I Googled 'rewards platform Bitcointalk' and 'rewards network Bitcointalk' to scout out similar altcoins, and found a slew of stuff that, though not exactly the same, shared some characteristics with Bytecent. Some are pre-ICO announcements, which we will ignore here, but established projects like Steem and Experience Points, and less established projects like Circuits of Value and Yoyow, popped up. Steem has a market cap of 82,877BTC (468x the market cap of BYC); Experience Points has a market cap of 8913BTC (50x the market cap of BYC); Yoyow has a market cap of 3008BTC (17x the market cap of BYC); and Circuits of Value has a market cap of 1270BTC (7x the market cap of BYC). Each of these projects is valued higher, at varying degrees, than Bytecent, but share a number of similarities with it.

Where this becomes useful for exits is in the comparison of these similar coins. Of the four, Experience Points (XP) is most alike to Bytecent but is valued 50x higher. Now, undoubtedly this is partly to do with development and community, as well as exchange exposure (though BYC has the additional advantage of trading on Bittrex, unlike XP), but, given even a brief evaluation of the fundamentals of the two projects, it becomes evident that Bytecent can quite easily be trading at a market cap akin to that of Experience Points, especially when you consider that Bytecent has no premine and is still achieving impressive goals. We can use the valuation of XP as a *possible* future valuation, there or thereabouts, for Bytecent, since the two have comparable traits.

Of course, 5000% growth is rarely a short-term deal, but, if I was accumulating BYC at its current price, I would incorporate market cap evaluation into my exit strategy: specifically, 10% of every position I am in is held for the possibility that it grows to the valuation of a larger, similar altcoin. Further, I combine this with technical analysis by pairing levels of support and resistance or Fibonacci extensions with the corresponding market cap valuation at those price-levels. This is done to find levels of confluence, where technical targets align with the potential fundamental valuation of any given alt relative to its peers. So, in the case of Bytecent, I would be looking for technical reasoning that complements the possibility of it reaching the same market cap as Experience Points. If I find such confluence, I put aside 5-10% of my position (the exact amount is dependent on the strength of the technical analysis relative to the feasibility of the potential valuation). This can be called a 'moonbag'. Another portion of my position is kept as a moonbag but on the basis of a volume-based exit, which we will get into in the next section.

Exchanges

Exchanges might seem, at first glance, to be somewhat unrelated to the fundamentals of a coin, but there are subtleties to this aspect of a project that have consequences for growth, outside of the evident pump-on-listing effect we see when a large exchange announces the addition of a new coin. In fact, exchanges offer us another exit target for our longer-term positions, in a way not too dissimilar from the market cap exit approach I meandered through in the previous section.

The number of exchanges in existence seems to have grown in accordance with the growth we have seen in the creation of cryptocurrencies, and while there are well over a hundred exchanges in operation, there are only really a handful I concern myself with. These are as follows, in order of average 24-hour volume:

Binance; Bittrex; Poloniex; KuCoin; Livecoin; Cryptopia; CoinExchange; CryptoBridge.

And of those eight, it is only really Bittrex, Cryptopia and Coinexchange that I find myself logging into on a regular basis. Each of these exchanges has its own characteristics, and these characteristics provide insight into the fundamental grounds for opening a new position. With regards to the research process, I tend to filter for coins that are already trading on one of these eight exchanges, since each occupies a slightly different space on the spectrum of volume.

Most new coins will find themselves first listed on CryptoBridge or CoinExchange, and the aim tends to be to climb the volume ladder through Cryptopia and Livecoin onto KuCoin and Poloniex, and eventually, if they are lucky, gain a prestigious listing on Binance or Bittrex. What can be observed through this progression is exponential growth, and I first discover many of my microcap picks listed on the three lowest volume exchanges of the eight (primarily Cryptopia, to be honest). This is where accumulation begins. Naturally, the more volume exposure a coin can get, the larger its market cap tends to be: to elaborate, the lowest market cap that can be found on Binance is around 2900BTC ($30mn), which means there are no lowcaps or microcaps at all on that exchange, and on Bittrex the lowest market cap is around 170BTC ($2mn). Compare this to Cryptopia, which has a multitude of alts below a 25BTC ($265k) market cap. The goldmine exists in the lower-volume exchanges.

One strategy to employ using this information is rather simple. When you find a coin that holds its own, fundamentally and technically, as per the methods of evaluation in these chapters, enter a position and preserve 5% of it to see out the progression through exchanges. If you've done your research thoroughly enough, the likelihood is that the altcoin you've accumulated will, at some point, make its way through the ranks. I do this for every new coin I enter that is not a short-term play. Anything that I'm looking to hold onto for longer than a month, I set aside 5% of that position – similarly to the portion I set aside for a market cap exit – and hold onto it, distributing 1-2% with each larger exchange that the coin finds itself listed on. This is a great way to ensure that you garner the greatest reward for your research and your patience whilst also adhering to the critical rule of taking partial profits (as we shall come onto later) as the coin – and thus, the position – grows in value.

There is another exit strategy that can be employed based on the exchange that a coin is listed on, and it is more concerned with coins that are already listed on larger exchanges (and so, cannot benefit from exchange progression in the same way), or for true shitcoin plays, where one is seeking to profit from the pump-and-dump cycles that **every** altcoin experiences periodically. I adopted this approach from Ant, a friend of mine in the space (@thisisnuse on Twitter). He and I were talking about exit strategies and periodic profit-taking throughout a bull cycle, and he mentioned that he uses the 24-hour volume as an indicator for when to sell a portion of his position. The premise is that each exchange facilitates a certain amount of volume, and, to get into the top 5 or 10 coins on an exchange by 24-hour volume, that coin must reach a certain level of volume itself. Using Bittrex as an example, to get into the top 5 coins by traded volume today, a coin would need to surpass 1900BTC. To get into the top 10, it would need to surpass 1200BTC. Now, for the top 50 coins by market cap, this level of traded volume over a 24-hour period is nothing special, but for the microcaps and lowcaps – and even the midcaps – that we are concerning ourselves with, this would be phenomenal.

The point is that merely by being listed on Bittrex, a coin is in an environment in which such volume is possible. For the coins that we are looking to accumulate, reaching the top 5 or even top 10 for 24-hour volume would be a leading indicator for the nearing of the peak of that particular bull/pump cycle, as this volume would be well out of the norm and would displace the regular highcap occupiers of these positions. Thus, the exit strategy is to reserve a small percentage of the position for the possibility that the coin reaches this level of volume, and then to exit that percentage if and when that is achieved. I have found this approach, and the theory behind it, to be very useful in my own speculation, and it has provided another exit avenue that is extricable from technical analysis. The larger the toolbox, and the more extensive our understanding of the tools, the better equipped we are to make successive profitable trades.

Block Explorers and Rich-Lists

The one aspect of my approach to fundamental analysis
that I am most often asked about is on the subject of the
block explorer, and how I use the information provided to
better understand the growth potential of a coin. In my
experience, there is no other asset class that is illuminated
with such transparency as cryptocurrencies, and the block
explorer is one of the tools unique to the cryptosphere that
is most insightful for a speculator. It is the most important
tool outside of a chart for monitoring and analysing the
workings of smart-money, and **that** is the key to
understanding a market and profiting from it. Of course,
the other aspects of fundamental analysis that deal with
the structural underpinnings of a project are incredibly
important in building an overall picture, but we are
traders who are looking to exploit the market, and thus
our focus should always be on figuring out price;
understanding the market-maker **is** understanding the
market.

The feature of the block explorer that we are most
concerned with is the *rich-list*. This is simply a list of the
singular addresses with the largest holdings in a coin, and
is rendered by the transparency of the blockchain.
Depending on the service used to host the block explorer,
or its unique layout, the rich-list may appear in different
forms. In the majority of cases, it appears simply as 'Rich
List', as per any block explorer hosted on Chainz, such as
the Blackcoin (BLK) explorer – https://chainz.cryptoid.info/
blk/#!rich. It can also appear as a 'Top 100' tab on other

explorers, such as the Condensate (RAIN) explorer – http://condensate.io/richlist. Note that on the Chainz explorers, it is the 'Rich List' that you want, rather than the 'Largest Wallets' tab. The latter is much more confusing to navigate and less useful for our purposes. The rich-list is what we want, as it displays singular addresses and the activity of each, making it easier to analyse.

Specifically, what the rich-list allows us to figure out is the pattern and extent of accumulation or distribution of the coin. What I mean by that is that, by tracking the activity of these top addresses, one can assess whether the coin is being stockpiled at current prices, thus making a stronger case for our own accumulation, or whether the coin is being sold by the large holders, thus providing us with potential reasoning for exiting at least part of our position.

Before I get into the specifics of my approach, I think it's important to note the relationship between accumulation and distribution on the block explorer, and on the chart. What I have noticed is that rich-list analysis is most effective when used in conjunction with the chart, as accumulation is most readily and easily observed when a coin is at cyclical lows and distribution when it is at the highs. Whilst this may seem a somewhat obvious point, rich-list analysis can throw you off if this is not kept in mind.

For example, I have witnesses top addresses seemingly reducing their positions in a coin despite that coin being at cyclical lows **and** long-term support. This sounds counter-intuitive at first – why would smart-money be dumping their coins at the least profitable price? And surely, if the top addresses are selling here, I shouldn't be buying? These are questions I asked myself when I first began utilising the block explorer in my analysis, but there are several explanations for this behaviour. Firstly, there are times when large holders are simply looking to reduce exposure due to their vast positions, regardless of the price they are selling at. This tends to happen in periods of general market unrest and uncertainty. The other explanation is that the market-makers in that coin have already profited from numerous bull cycles and are now cleansing the final portions of their position, as can be observed by continued distribution from those addresses over a prolonged period, which you can match up with the time-frame on the corresponding chart to find out at what prices the majority of the position was distributed. In these cases, what is usually happening is a changeover of smart-money. Now, this does not have to be co-ordinated (and I doubt it usually is), but what I have often spotted in such scenarios is the top few addresses distributing at the lows, and the addresses just below them in the rich-list aggressively increasing their positions, thus eventually overtaking them as the new whales.

However, outside of what I just described, the general rule I use is **buy when the top addresses are increasing their positions and sell when the top addresses are decreasing their positions**. As I say, this will almost always correspond with the former taking place at the lows on a chart, and the latter at the highs.

Note: I realise I must have mentioned 'lows' and 'highs' on the chart somewhat vaguely a number of times in this book without explaining what that is for those who are inexperienced with charts, but I promise that will all be covered in the *Technical Analysis* chapter.

So, how exactly do I spot and track accumulation and distribution and use that to my advantage? It is really rather simple, and just requires patience and discipline – no sophisticated strategy necessary. For the sake of clarity, I will refer to the Blackcoin explorer I mentioned earlier in this section. My method is as follows:

1. Direct your browser to the block explorer of your choice. In this example, I am using https://chainz.cryptoid.info/blk/#!rich.
2. Screenshot the page so that you can see the top 10 addresses and their amounts. Save this image to a folder for Blackcoin (or whichever coin you are analysing) and date it.
3. Open up a new tab for each of the top 10 addresses.
4. Despite worry of condescension, the (+) transactions you see are accumulation (either, through buying or mining) and the (-) transactions are distribution (or perhaps transfers).
5. Evaluate the most recent transaction history of all of these top 10 addresses, and note down how many of them seem to be, on balance, in accumulation, and how many are reducing their positions. What you will tend to find is the majority of the top 10

addresses in accumulation when a coin is at the lows on the chart, and vice-versa. But make sure you note this down rather than try to remember.

6. Now, repeat this process every day or two for a couple of weeks. Screenshot the rich-list front page, and then note down what is required from the top 10 addresses each time. This is your smart-money blueprint.

7. Using the data you have compiled, observe the changes taking place in the rich-list, and assess whether, on balance, the smart-money seems to be in accumulation across the period of analysis. If you find that the larger addresses seem to be adding to their position, this is a very good indicator that you should also be accumulating at these prices.

8. For distribution, this process is essentially reversed, except that you monitor for distribution every day for a week, since distribution occurs faster than accumulation (as can be observed on a chart). You want to see the majority of the top addresses begin to reduce their position over this period, and this implies that a peak is nearing, and thus you should also be selling.

That is the process in its entirety. I have found it to be incredibly insightful, deepening my understanding of the market-maker of any given coin, and thus allowing for more successful speculation. This is the least fundamental of all the fundamental analysis, and almost seems as if it belongs within technical analysis, but it is simply a fundamental approach to understanding price-action.

Community

The heart and soul of any cryptocurrency is its community, as is the heart and soul of the cryptosphere itself. An altcoin without a strong core of supporters never seems to survive the accelerated market cycles in this space. It is the foundational strength that has allowed for a multitude of coins to survive numerous pump-and-dumps and near-death experiences, and to be reborn, rebuilt and revitalised. I can recall several occasions in 2014 where coins would be abandoned by their developer but the existence of a committed community prevented those coins from fading away. Somewhat floral prose aside, a community **is** the bedrock of a coin, and will make certain that our trades and investments do not wither away into non-existence. For that reason alone, it is integral to our fundamental analysis.

For the purposes of community analysis, I am looking at two things: social media presence and Bitcointalk thread activity. Community analysis, in this respect, is pretty straightforward, but it allows us to gauge the legitimacy of an altcoin. And this is significant for risk allocation prior to opening a new position, as we will get into in the *Risk and Portfolio Management* section.

Social media presence is perhaps the more significant of these two, as social media unquestionably plays such a critical part in so much of our lives now, extending well beyond the cryptosphere. It is beginning to surpass traditional advertising and has been proven to be a more effective form of marketing for all manner of things; cryptocurrencies are no different, in this respect. For the majority, social media platforms – be it Twitter, Telegram or Facebook (or a host of other platforms) – are where one first encounters new coins and where one frequents in order to keep up to date with already-established coins. Thus, these platforms provide the foundation for communities to be built around a project and allow for mass growth in user-base.

A growing community has a number of effects on price: the first is an obvious one, as a growing community means more individuals buying into the coin and this injects volume into the market; secondly, the more individuals involved in the coin – the more people talking about it and assisting with it in whatever ways they can – the higher the probability that that project does not die, as members of the community would be there to step in and replace team members who might leave, which allows for long-term reliability; lastly, social media is exceptionally viral, and projects that focus much of their attention on **organically** increasing their social media presence tend to benefit from the more widespread attention, thus attracting new market participants, as community growth via these platforms is exponential, not linear.

Gauging the strength of a coin's social media presence is very simple, and just requires some time. I begin by finding all of the social platforms that a coin is on, and the most common of these are Twitter, Facebook, Telegram, Discord and Slack. You should be able to find these via their websites or their Bitcointalk announcement threads. Once I have a list of these platform links, I join them all, and do a quick, surface-level figure count: followers, group members – that sort of thing. Note these all down, but be aware that these can be misleading due to fake follower purchases and spam content etc. Following this, I spend a few hours sequentially going through each of the platforms and monitoring the quality of the conversation on them. I'm looking for little to no spam; active chat between the members of the groups, ideally on the subject of the project itself, such as ideas being thrown back and forth or the discussion of current development and price-action; useful or informative posts by developers (or their admins); interaction and engagement levels on tweets and Facebook posts etc. In short, I am evaluating these platforms to discern whether there is genuine interest in the coin. There are no real metrics by which I measure this – it must be palpable.

Bitcointalk was once the hub of all altcoin activity, but as social media platforms came to the forefront – and coins began to fund professional websites of their own as opposed to the awful, half-broken websites developers would throw up in 2014 – the forum has fallen by the wayside a little, but I happen to still use it just as much today as I did back then. In fact, if a coin doesn't have a Bitcointalk announcement, I won't even bother with it. The announcement thread is the page that provides all the necessary information I need to determine whether a coin is worth further research, so, if there isn't one, I'm not going to waste time in attempting to discover this information elsewhere.

Aside from this initial insight, the forum acts as another channel on which we can evaluate the strength of the community. I utilise it in a similar way to social media platforms, in that I am monitoring the quality of conversation to assess whether this is a community that is committed to the coin, and one that is looking to assist where it can. Prior to accumulating a new position, I **always** check the coin's Bitcointalk ANN (announcement) for recent activity – no recent activity, likely no new trade. What I often find when researching coins is that their specs will be great, their market cap will be low, and then, as soon as I navigate to the ANN, there has been no communication from the devs or the community in months. This, to me, is a dead project, and it is discarded from the list. Of course, this filters out some projects that have merely migrated to other platforms, and may well be active, but once again the abundance of coins in the space allows for this to be inconsequential. For every one coin I may discard from the research list due to a lack of recent activity on their ANN, there will be five to ten others that have continued to utilise the forum.

After I have filtered for coins that **do** have continued conversation on these threads, I then read through a month's worth of recent posts, whether it be across three pages or thirty pages, monitoring how often new posts are being made, how many different individuals are posting (in order to get an idea for community size on Bitcointalk), and whether the posts are high in quality or not: no spam; project-focused conversation; and a commitment to the coin. One thing I have found useful about this process in particular is that, unlike on other platforms, any issues with the coin are easily identifiable, and any problems they have had in the past can be ascertained quickly. This is, in part, because unmoderated forums do not allow for posts to be deleted, so, if there have been developer issues or anything similar, these cannot be hidden. Also, Bitcointalk users just seem more vocal about problems, as will be evident by the slew of 'this is a scam' posts you will undoubtedly find when researching coins. In short, the threads are are a fantastic way to get a knowledge of the history of a coin, whilst evaluating community strength.

Development

The final section of this chapter on fundamental analysis will be focused on development, and the various ways in which this broad topic can be exploited to our advantage. Firstly, there are a few categories within development that I concern myself with, and these are: roadmaps + whitepapers; websites; wallets; and innovation. Within these four categories can be be found all the information one needs in order to assess growth potential, valuations and trade management.

Roadmaps + Whitepapers:

Whilst a whitepaper was a rarity for a new coin in 2014 (despite the existence of Satoshi's original whitepaper for Bitcoin), more recently, they have become all the rage, likely due to the ICO surge. Now, every single coin that launches seems to be including a whitepaper in their... roadmap, as though a whitepaper is some sort of achievement of development. However, I'm not one to complain, and admittedly this trend does come with many advantages. A whitepaper provides us, as speculators, with important information for our positions, and a deeper understanding of the vision of the developers is no bad thing. When combined with the roadmap, we are able to learn a little bit more about what can be expected from the team, and thus, whether we should be buying and where price may be going in the future.

Roadmaps: I'll begin with roadmaps, as they are simple to navigate and digest. A roadmap is merely a timeline or schedule of news and development, and they are often presented in the form of a visually-appealing graphic of some sort. For the purposes of this section, I will use the Shield (XSH) roadmap as an example, as I believe it is one of the most useful roadmaps I have seen: https://www.shieldx.sh/roadmap. At first glance, this might look less intuitive than some roadmaps you may have come across, in that it is not presented in the form of a chronological timeline of events. However, whilst that layout might be more visually-appealing, what we are looking for is easily digestible information on upcoming developments, and this is where the Shield roadmap excels. I look at a roadmap in the same way one is taught to write down goals for projects or businesses: the events on the roadmap must be specific, measurable, achievable, relevant and trackable, and each event must be clearly delineated or segmented so as to provide clarity on the progress and direction of the coin. A roadmap that is presented with these characteristics is one that can be used to assess the fundamental quality of the development, as well as the ambition of the project, and thus, becomes useful post-entry of a position, in particular, as one can view the progress being made by the team. From this, we can judge whether it is best to hold onto a position (and potentially how long to hold for) or to dump it and reinvest the capital elsewhere, as we know whether the team is falling short of their targets (or failing to meet them at all) or over-achieving.

Also, there may be future developments on the roadmap that are worth holding on for, given that the team are achieving current goals and targets; by this, I mean that there will be some coins that are looking to innovate or, as is more often the case, implement existing features that are valued highly by market participants, such as anonymity or masternodes – for example, POSWallet, which is developing Trust-less Staking. The appearance of these development goals on a roadmap can add expected future value to a project, which often manifests in sustained interest leading up to the implementation of these developments, and then in a surge in price when they are successfully implemented. I have witnessed this occur for a number of markets, predominantly for coins that implement an anonymity feature or masternodes, and so I pay greater attention to projects with these developments in their roadmaps.

It is a risky game to buy into a coin or hold an existing position based on perceived future value pending the success of specific developments, thus it is especially important that the **consistency** of the team is considered prior to placing any weight on these events. Any developer can add a host of trendy future features to a roadmap but very few follow through, and fewer still in a timely, consistent manner. This is also why it is useful when a roadmap contains some sort of measure of progress, as the Shield roadmap does. It allows us to see what has been completed, what is close to completion, what is in its early stages of development and what has yet to begin.

I realise I've been babbling on now for a few hundred words, and I've yet to elaborate on how exactly I use roadmaps to assist with trade management: firstly, I evaluate the possible value of an entry against the progress of the roadmap. Of course, as I have stressed numerous times throughout this chapter, I do not assess altcoins against sole facets of fundamental analysis, but rather weigh them all in conjunction to gain a fuller understanding of the various strengths and shortcomings of any given coin. But, I certainly do look at whether the developers are achieving their goals according to the schedules and deadlines that they have set themselves.

I use a simple scale from 1 to 5 for this purpose: a coin scores 1 if it has no roadmap; 2 if it has a vague, valueless roadmap, or deadlines are not being met whatsoever; 3 if it has a well-structured roadmap but is hit-and-miss with the targets that are set out; 4 if it has a complete, detailed roadmap but there has been more than one missed deadline; 5 if it has a perfect roadmap and has only ever missed one deadline, though ideally none. The higher the score, the stronger the case for entering a position. You want to be accumulating coins with teams that demonstrate high levels of productivity and consistency, in order to minimise downside risk. Price will be manipulated regardless of this, as I have stated before, but the coins that continually meet deadlines and make progress are the coins that do not die, and so, these positions can be held through bear markets with a reduced risk of them losing upwards of 90% of their value, as many alts do. The ability to hold a position for prolonged periods of time whilst minimising the downside risk of that position is what produces the greatest return-on-investment. These coins have a fundamental basis for retaining more of their value (relative to other coins) during bear cycles – independent of market manipulation – and this is why we see stronger buy support enter the market when these coins reach key technical levels, where fundamentally-weak coins may plunge through these levels with some ease.

Whitepapers: As for whitepapers, the premise is similar except that they are a little more dependent upon our intuition than much else. We are looking for conciseness, consistency, comprehensibility and no small amount of ambition: pages and pages of unbridled technical jargon are often used as a placeholder for substance, and too often will you find new coins that attempt to impress and attract new investors with a dense and lengthy whitepaper. In short, simplicity is key.

Whilst it tends to primarily be ICOs that employ the use of the whitepaper, there are many PoW or PoS coins that write one up, viewing it as a point-of-attraction for market participants, and thus we do need to pay some attention to them. For me, they aren't quite so important as the roadmap, as the critical information tends to be more clearly described on a roadmap than in a whitepaper – the whitepaper is the medium for depth rather than clarity, in my experience, and as a speculator, rather than a long-term member of the community (or user of the coin), I'm not overly concerned with the nitty-gritty details for the next decade of the coin's existence.

However, there is one primary detail that one often finds in a whitepaper that seems to be impossible to find anywhere else, and it harks back to a significant earlier section of the book: the premine. Where Bitcointalk threads are the go-to for determining the existence of a premine, the whitepaper is the go-to for determining where and how the team are intending to use these funds. I tend to err on the side of caution when it comes to premines, so this information plays a part in my decision-making. If the whitepaper can detail with some specificity what the premine is intended for, I am more than willing to forego my reservations and begin to look for a good entry. It is important to emphasise specificity, as any team can (and many teams do) just draw up a meaningless pie chart, depicting the various portions of the premine and their intended pathways.

I maintain, whitepapers are more about intuition than anything else – if your gut tells you that the section on premines does little to explain or justify the existence of the premine in the first place, or, worse yet, stirs in the stomach the feeling of suspicion, go with your gut. If your gut tells you that the premine seems justified, **listen**. Intuition is a magical thing, and it definitely grows to be more reliable with experience. Once you've researched fifty or a hundred or two hundred coins, you'll know what feels right. And I know that isn't what many will want to hear, as it implies extensive commitment is crucial, rather than there being some sort of system or strategy that produces proficiency, but, unlike its technical counterpart, there is much about the fundamental that is reliant upon your gut.

Websites:

There is an allure to a beautifully crafted website – one that can be navigated effortlessly and that presents information cleanly and concisely; one that just looks and feels pleasing. In 2014, there was an unsurprising lack of such websites, with most developers opting for cheap templates and sloppy text, if they created a website at all. However, following the explosion of interest in the space over the past eighteen months, there is now a plethora of coins with immaculate websites, as developers have learnt that this is the first point-of-reference for both, speculators and users alike. And it is indeed the case that in 2014 many of us would look towards Bitcointalk or Twitter to find out more about a coin, and now almost everyone is focusing their attention on its website.

But how are websites involved in my fundamental analysis? Well, the first thing I do is discard any coin from my research list that doesn't have a website. Why? Partly because it helps reduce what is always a tediously lengthy list, but predominantly due to a couple of assumptions that we can make about the absence of a website. As a website is, as we have already established, the first point-of-reference for the majority when they first become aware of a coin, it is undoubtedly a significant – if not the most significant – tool for building interest. If the team behind a coin are so unconcerned with building interest that they fail to create a website of any kind, they do not deserve our attention as speculators, because a team that neglects this aspect of development is not one that is generally conducive to the growth of the coin – either in community or price – and tends to be incompetent (in my experience) at other aspects of development. No website means no central source of detailed information about the project, and thus, tends to manifest in smaller communities being established around the coin. This, as you will remember from the section on community, is not ideal. We want popularity; sustained interest; commitment. In short, I equate the absence of a website with ineffective, insufficient development, which can lead to a lack of community growth, and thus limited fundamental strength, or higher risk on our positions. Those are the assumptions I make when I come across a coin with no website, and that is why they are immediately discarded, even if it means I miss out on a handful of potentially solid projects.

So, we've cleared out another swarm of projects, but, of the ones that do have a website, how can we determine which are the best to pursue? The obvious parallels are there to be drawn between roadmaps and websites, in that you are essentially looking for similar things from both: conciseness, substance, ease-of-use and attractiveness. I employ a similar scale system for evaluating websites, where 1 is the absence of a website, and 5 is the most immaculate, responsive and thorough website. A coin with a 1 is discarded from the list, and a coin with a 5 is considered more highly for potential accumulation. Beyond that, there is little else that need be said on the subject. Onto meatier topics.

Wallets:

Wallets form the spine of any cryptocurrency project, and while I won't wax philosophical about the benefits of a wallet over a traditional bank account here, it is something that needs emphasising. Without the invention of the wallet (in the context of cryptocurrency), we'd all still be transacting at the pace and cost of the current financial system. Thus, wallets are integral to our fundamental analysis.

There are a multitude of ways to approach the analysis, but I'd like to begin with the existence of different types of wallet. Where, in traditional finance, you have a bank account (be it a current or savings account, the difference between these is negligible) to store your fiat, or you have cash, in crypto we are provided with a greater range of means by which to store our coins. You can use paper wallets, local wallets, web wallets, mobile wallets, hardware wallets, or even exchanges. All of these function in a similar way, with regards to transactions, but have different features and certainly different advantages and disadvantages. And, on the topic of local wallets, you also have different operating systems for which the wallets are specifically created. When confronted with such breadth of choice, one thing becomes quite obvious: the **potential** user-base of cryptocurrencies is superior to that of a bank. Anyone with an internet connection can be catered for in one way or another – and, in fact, you would only need an internet connection once to generate a paper wallet, so this increases the potential user-base beyond those who **own** devices with an internet connection.

So, how is this insightful for a speculator? As I mentioned in *Community*, a coin with the largest possible potential user-base is something we want to see, as the scope for community growth is maximised. Therefore, something I tend to look out for is the existence of as many forms of wallets as possible. It's just not good enough to have a Windows wallet, a Linux wallet and an exchange listing. Of course, for brand-new coins, it is unfair to expect all the potential forms of wallets to be developed immediately (though, there are developers who do the background work for a lot of this prior to launching their coins – keep an eye out for those coins). However, I do filter my research list based on either current or pending wallets.

For example, let's say I have found a coin when poring over Coinmarketcap that possesses many of the characteristics I look for in its specification – call it CF. CF looks promising at the surface-level, but when I dig deeper into its website and its announcement thread, I find that only a Windows and a Linux wallet has been developed. There is no paper wallet, no Mac wallet, no mobile wallet and no web wallet – exchange listings aren't a deal-breaker and support on hardware wallets is unlikely for the majority of microcaps or lowcaps. Now, a mobile wallet might be asking for a bit much, but a web wallet, a paper wallet and a Mac wallet should be standard practice for developers. In the announcement thread, I also find no schedule for the release of these wallets, so I have little to go on with regards to the expectation of a fully-fledged range for potential users. All of this suggests that the potential user-base of CF is limited to Windows and Linux users who want (or have the faculty) to store their coins locally on their computers. Limited potential user-base implies a lower chance of CF growing its community and gaining traction, and thus, I'm now looking at a coin that might be good to play for a possible pump-and-dump, but certainly not one I would be looking to accumulate a larger, more long-term position in. CF would then be placed on a 'one to watch' list, in case development does pick up, but it would not be a coin I focus my attention on.

There is, naturally, a caveat to this approach. Is the coin offering something more than the standard altcoin? Have the team suggested that development is underway for something henceforth unseen or uncommon in crypto? If the answer to these questions is yes – and there will be coins you find in your research process that are more unique than others – then a total disregard of such a coin on the basis of its lack of choice of wallets would seem unreasonable. In these rare but real cases, I do utilise a little more risk, as the upside of potentially groundbreaking projects is too great to neglect, and thus they would remain in the core list. Regular alts do not get this privilege. Potential user-base is paramount, and a limited wallet choice is not something I can get on board with.

Where else can we find some insight from wallets to aid in our speculation? Well, we can go a little bit more micro. Let us consider the local wallet, which is arguably the cornerstone of wallet development. The local wallet is where most of us hold our positions; where we make many of our transactions; where we stake and where we run our masternodes. It is the hub of activity for the smart speculator – I say 'smart' because there are many who hold the majority of their crypto-wealth on exchanges, which is **always** a terrible idea. Thus, I'm sure you'll agree, the necessity for an optimal local wallet is critical.

But where does this come into play with regards to trading? Much of the importance is indirect, and relates more to the security of your altcoins (and the feasibility of transactions) than it does to trade execution. And though it may sound a bit of a bore, security is no joke, and neither is potential non-functionality, so let's not just glide over that. Nobody wants to transfer the position they've spent weeks accumulating to a poorly-built wallet to find that the wallet crashes every time they try to make a transaction, and trust me it happens. Far too many wallets consume an exorbitant amount of memory to run, and, by doing so, become virtually unusable for many. The security of local wallet storage becomes less attractive if the local wallet can't send a transaction without frying your circuit board. As such, any coin I am looking to pick up must have a fully-functional wallet for my operating system and must run smoothly. To this end, I tend to download a coin's wallet and buy a small amount to play around with. This may seem a waste of time to some but it's something that makes me feel more comfortable about potentially large positions, and that is invaluable when you consider the psychology of trade management: bad trading decisions are made in abundance by those who don't know how to manage risk or control their emotions, now add to that the additional stress of your position being stored in a wallet you haven't properly tested, or that you have tested only to find that it struggles to function. Consider the potential gains that could be lost (or capital that could be failed to be preserved) by a failed transaction at the opportune (or ill-timed) moment. I don't wish to take on those risks, and so, a coin without a functioning local wallet is a no-go, except in the rare case that there is hardware wallet support. Give yourself some peace of mind and stick to the above.

Innovation:

Ah, the promised land of development. The projects that have a genuine chance of growing 100x tend to be ones that exhibit some of the traits or features that we'll be going into in this section. Innovation is inherent and ubiquitous in the cryptosphere, with no shortage of never-before-seen developments being thought up and built on a regular basis. Innovation is a diamond-mine of profitability, and the much-revered, near-mythical 10000% gain that speculators in this space yearn for is made possible, in part, because of this.

Having been the fortunate beneficiary of a handful of 100x trades myself, I can understand why the questions I am most often asked run along the lines of, 'what are your thoughts on so-and-so for a potential 100x?' or 'which coins are on your radar for a 100x?' The idea that there is the chance for one's life to be changed on the basis of just one trade is somewhat incomprehensible, but it is a legitimate opportunity in crypto, and one that is not even all that uncommon, and that in itself is something of a miracle for those seeking financial freedom.

However, whilst this opportunity is not uncommon, it is incredibly difficult to capitalise on, and even if I answered those messages I get asking which coin I think is most likely to experience such growth, the majority of the individuals asking those questions simply would not have the intestinal fortitude or the titanium testicles that it requires to buy a microcap at the lows and hold it through the hurricane of fear, uncertainty and doubt that is inevitable on the road to the 10000% return.

Anyway, I digress, but the point is that these opportunities are certainly present, and I have found that they almost exclusively reside in one domain – undervalued innovation. And that is what I am most often looking for when researching altcoins, but rarely is it found. Usually, the scenario is such where I find a coin that sounds very promising on the innovation front, but scores poorly everywhere else, and these I keep an eye on but feel some frustration at the fact that my experience won't allow for me to just jump in and buy. Extreme undervaluation can lend itself to a 100x without the need for innovation, as I found with Neutron, when I bought it at 150 satoshis and it peaked around 18000 satoshis. This coin wasn't reinventing the wheel, not at that time, anyway, but they were doing all of the simple things incredibly well, and thus I saw the opportunity for extreme growth.

However, my view is that the fuel that is required for such extreme growth – aside from the tears of newbies jumping into pumps without a second thought – *is* that reinvention of the wheel, or the creation of an entirely new structure itself. It is the excitement of the novel, the distinction and triumph of breaking new ground, that I think affords market-makers the capacity to run a microcap up into the top 100 coins. Without that fervour about a coin, the job is much more difficult, since there are fewer willing to buy the bag at the top of a shitcoin pump than there are for a project that has continued to exhibit innovative qualities.

So, what am I looking for when searching out undervalued innovation? The truth is, it's not always actually originality, as the ubiquity of dumb money allows for the undervaluation of what was previously innovative but now omnipresent to reap similar rewards, time and time again. And I don't mean that to come across harshly – it is simply a matter of fact that for every tweet you see of someone boasting of their 20x or 50x or 100x win, there is likely some poor sod somewhere beating his fists against the wall and setting his laptop on fire since, more likely than not, his investment will now retrace 90% from his buys at the top. Which do you want to be, the former or the latter? As unpleasant as it may be, everyone wants to be the former, and, for that to happen, the latter must exist.

The point I began to make was that, due to the scarcity of genuinely groundbreaking projects, we simply need to look for projects that are doing what was once innovative exceptionally well, or that are tweaking and improving previous originality, in the same way your local garage might replace your intake to get a little bit more out of your car. These projects are far more numerous, and they are often cheap.

Before we get onto the specifics of what I look for, there is another useful truth about the space that I'd like to share: the market has, of late, begun to form sectoral trends. What I mean by this is that, back in 2014, the altcoin market would pump either randomly or as one singular entity, but nowadays we are seeing more and more evidence of small sectors of coins growing disproportionately to the rest of the existing coins, outperforming the entire market at times, and these sectors are predominantly grounded in innovative features. Find the feature that is going to become part of a trend and you can get in on a wave of pumps within one small category of coins. These sectors tend to comprise of the various features or protocols I look for when researching alts: primarily, masternodes, staking and anonymity. Other features exist and are being developed (and this is often where real innovation is found, as I will discuss a little later) but these three form the foundation for sectoral bull runs, and for the majority of coins that experience truly considerable growth.

Staking/Masternodes: Of the three, masternodes and staking are the most straightforward features and very much go hand-in-hand, so I'll begin with them. Masternodes are merely designated collateral that is held in a wallet to assist with numerous functions on the blockchain, and, as an incentive for fulfilling these functions, masternode holders are rewarded with part of the block reward. For any cryptographer that may be reading, I probably butchered that definition, but that's the basic premise and is all we need to know for speculative purposes. Staking works in a similar way, except a little simpler: any amount of a coin with the capacity to be staked can be held in a wallet and, simply by the act of leaving the wallet open, these coins will be rewarded – usually with a fixed annual percentage – like interest in a bank account. For those previously unaware or unsure of these concepts, the lightbulb in your head should be glowing bright right now, as you realise that these two features offer the opportunity to make passive gains on your positions. This is the most obvious advantage to concentrating your capital on coins that have these features, and it produces a number of positive effects for your trade management:

1. The rewards reaped from staking or running a masternode can be sold to provide bitcoin for new positions or for passive income. I tend not to adopt this approach all that often, in all honesty, due to the following effects.
2. Rewards that aren't sold immediately for the above reasons add to your position without incurring any

real cost to you. This reduces the average price of your position, which reduces your risk (which here means the likelihood of a profitable trade) whilst simultaneously increasing your exposure (the size of your position) and thus your potential gains.

3. These rewards can also function as a hedge during bear markets. Most coins fall off significantly during their bear cycles, but having positions in strong stakers or particularly profitable masternodes can offset how underwater your position may be. This also functions as weak-hand prevention; if you're new to the space and unused to the extreme volatility of these markets, having positions that are producing rewards whilst being 50% or further underwater can aid in stopping you from selling at a loss. When accumulated with proper risk management, positions in masternode and staking coins can minimise the likelihood of a losing trade, and, even in the case of a losing trade, this loss is reduced by the increase in position size from the rewards.

Now, this all may sound too good to be true, and, when not approached correctly, it is. There is one big red flag that stands out here: **liquidity**. Will the coin you've accumulated continue to have sufficient liquidity for the rewards it is providing? This is a very important question to consider, as improper analysis can leave you with a bag that you are unable to liquidate regardless of the mass passive gains a coin may promise. There is a great deal of profit to be made through the utility of these coins, but the inherently greater inflationary pressures that they suffer relative to other alts is something that must not be overlooked, and is something I consider heavily prior to any considerations of the potential benefits.

Liquidity becomes much more of a concern when the coin offers very high rewards. It doesn't take a mathematician to work out that, if a coin is offering 1000% annual staking rewards, there is the possibility for that coin's circulating supply to increase ten-fold over the course of a year.

Note: I always assume the maximum possible inflation in my analysis of staking or masternode coins, so that I am best prepared for the worst possible scenario.

Thus, assuming that there is no 'burn' mechanism, there may well need to be an equivalent increase in demand for the coin to sustain current price levels. The likelihood is that, instead of demand keeping up with such a large increase in supply, price will simply dilute and diminish over the twelve-month period, and the position you accumulated at the beginning of the year (for the purposes of gaining these staking rewards) is now actually worth a similar amount of bitcoin or less despite growing in size.

From this point, there would be a couple of possibilities: you would either have to wait it out and hope that the twelve months of patience and locked away capital will result in the coin pumping and allowing for an exit of greater value than that of your initial position, or you dump and recoup what you can since you didn't factor in the inflationary pressure of the rewards. However, this is not always possible, thanks to liquidity (or a lack thereof). What you may find is that the 1000% annual staking rewards lead to a dramatic reduction in the buy support for a coin, as demand fails to keep up with supply, and not only do you find that price reduces, but also the option for an exit can disappear when you're dealing with the high-risk, lower-liquidity realm of microcaps and lowcaps. So, I've outlined the potential risks and pitfalls of incorporating staking or masternode coins into your portfolio, but I maintain that the benefits I mentioned earlier in the section can outweigh these, given proper research and analysis.

Often what you will find is that masternode coins come conjoined with staking, and the option is there for you to utilise either (or both). I won't go into the mechanics of how these tools can be set up, since this isn't a tech-focused book, but a simple Google search will provide you with countless tutorials on both. What I want to elaborate on is my process of research and analysis for these coins, in particular, as there are some things that crop up that do not in my analysis for other kinds of projects. Firstly, I'd like you to recall the section on inflation, because those calculations are even more important here. When dealing with potentially enormous levels of inflation, it is paramount to have these figures worked out beforehand, so, for every staking or masternode project I am considering accumulating, I make certain to know what I can expect from the circulating supply, and thus the price, over the following months. I do have a stipulation or filter for these projects too, much like I do with other projects; any altcoin offering over 200% is an immediate no-go, because the likelihood that demand can keep up with the increase in supply over a long enough period of time to not only reap the rewards but also for there to be explosive price growth **and** the opportunity for exit is extremely slim, in my experience. These projects usually come and go within a three-month period. So, those are instantly off the list. We're not looking for projects that put us at a high risk of becoming 'community members', as the saying goes. We want longevity and security – the ability to reap the rewards to grow our positions (thus lowering our average entries and protecting us partially against downside risks), whilst not having to concern ourselves a great deal with the larger levels of inflation, and whilst also exhibiting the promise and the traits of future price growth that we look for from every other alt. That's the golden goose. And how exactly do we find the goose?

Well, for masternodes specifically, I have one simple calculation I make to assess the strength of the project, in the context of its masternode network. Most masternode projects will be listed on some form of ranking or statistic website, such as www.mnrank.com or www.masternodes.pro, and the statistics provided here can be insightful. Take Neutron, for example. Using the data on the latter website, we can see the number of masternodes currently online, the number of NTRN required to run a masternode, and the cost of 1 NTRN. Now, remember that market caps can be flimsy and unreliable in many respects, but what cannot be refuted is the value of a masternode network. In order to run a masternode, that collateral **must** be purchased and held. So, if we take the 25,000 NTRN requirement for a masternode and multiply it by the current value of 1 NTRN, we get a cost of around $3000 for a Neutron masternode. There are currently 386 Neutron masternodes online, so to find the value of Neutron's masternode network, we multiply the number of online masternodes by the cost of one masternode to get $1,158,000. There is over a million dollars worth of Neutron that has been bought and is currently locked away. Then, if we take the circulating market cap of Neutron, which, according to Coinmarketcap, is around $4m, Neutron's masternode network is around a quarter of the value of its market cap. This is a moderately valuable masternode network, and thus one that can likely be relied on for our longer-term trades or investments. If you make these calculations for all of the masternode coins you are considering, you'll get a spectrum of values to assess them by. Some projects might have exceptionally strong masternode networks, where over two-thirds of the value of their market caps have actually been bought and used to run masternodes, and some will have weak masternode networks, where the value is less than 10%. I use these values as a basis for assessment and further evaluation, tending to ignore any coins that come up with a value below 10%. All of these small filters allow for long lists of coins to be whittled down into a handful (or a few handfuls) of projects that display all the signs of strength and promise necessary for me to begin accumulating a position.

As for staking coins, my method of evaluation is less mathematical, as no comparable calculation can be made like that of the masternode network value. I do filter for coins that offer between 10-200% annually, as that has been the sweet-spot range for me, and instead I rely on the aspects of fundamental analysis that I have already covered to value the remaining stakers. What is especially important when looking at these projects is to consider where you think they are going in the future; whether they have a strong community and a hard-working team. In short, you want to analyse them for potential longevity, since positions that are accumulated and staked will need to be held for at least a few months to really reap the rewards. This is simply a matter of using what I have already talked about with regards to fundamental analysis and applying it to a greater degree – because of the inherently larger levels of inflation associated with staking coins, the fundamentals need to be that much stronger to ensure that demand is sustained over the period you are looking to hold your position for, as well as to allow for explosive price growth in the future. Market-makers have a tougher job when constructing a pump for staking coins, as, though they have the benefit of staking large positions they may have accumulated, more capital is required to move the market and to provide liquidity because of this, and thus it is a riskier play. I pay much more attention to the activity of rich-lists for staking coins than any other type of coin for this reason, because you need to be especially aware of what the larger holders are doing to avoid getting trapped in a position.

The flip-side for this harks back to the opening paragraphs of this section – staking and masternodes are formerly innovative features that **still** hold the attention of the masses, and continue to be at the forefront of bull-runs for this reason. There is palpable excitement when projects announce the implementation of masternodes, in particular, and this excitement is pump-fuel. Be cautious and calculated but confident when accumulating stakers and masternode coins and, in my experience, any wins you have in this sector will often far outshine other positions.

Anonymity: Where stakers and masternodes are exciting for us, the traders and investors, as they provide passive income and the opportunity to minimise risk and maximise reward, anonymity protocols are where the most utility can be found for the most people, and, as the coins that develop and implement anonymity have the largest potential user-bases, thus they have the highest potential for exponential growth. There is a great fervour surrounding anonymity tech in the space, with coins like Monero and Zcash leading the charge, but the real opportunity lies in the less-established anonymous coins. It is in this sector, in particular, that one can find and exploit extreme undervaluation, with a large number of microcaps and lowcaps exhibiting all the promising traits found in the highcaps, just with far more upside. Now, as I've made very clear in this book, I am but a technical Neanderthal, and, as such, it would simply reveal inadequacy were I to go into any level of depth on the various anonymity developments that currently exist or are being worked on. However, what will be of use to you, I hope, is a run-down of my process of elimination (or selection) from the plethora of projects working on this tech.

Parallels can certainly be drawn between the research and analysis process for masternode and anonymity coins – we are looking for similar qualities from both, as the positions we build in them are longer-term. Anonymity sells, but it takes time, since this is where we can find the projects that can potentially crack the top 200 or even 100 coins on Coinmarketcap from their humble beginnings in the microcap category. In general, it will probably take two or three bull cycles rather than one before your position reaches the dizzying gains in the five-digit percentage range, unless you happen to get in at the inception of a coin, so we're looking at well over twelve months of holding in many cases.

What I find helpful when whittling down anonymity coins is to segment them by the tech: most coins are forks or clones of other coins, and so, the anonymity features they have implemented (or are working on implementing) will already be existent elsewhere in the space, and any projects working on original tech would form their own sector. Split your anonymity coins up by these protocols, and then do a comparison within each sector as to how far into development the coins are; whether the tech is already integrated or whether there is a lot of work left to be done; how reliable or temperamental the tech is. I tend to use roadmaps and social media channels to answer these questions, as issues and flaws tend to be flagged rather swiftly in this space.

What I like to do from here is pick one or two coins from each sector – one with working tech and one where it is in the works – and begin to accumulate these. How do I pick? I use rich-list analysis, market cap evaluation, assessment of supply and inflation, and all the other tools I've gone into to form an opinion on which of these coins seems the most undervalued, relative to the others (and to the established highcap versions of itself, if those exist, which, in most cases, they do). It's a fairly simplistic process of selection, but I find that it spreads the risk in the portfolio between the projects in development (which are inherently more risky, but potentially more rewarding) and the projects that already have solid anonymity integration, whilst allowing for exposure to the maximum range of anonymity tech available in the space, so that, if one protocol in particular becomes 'trendy' and begins to take off, I have a position. You never know what might be the Monero or Dash of the years to come.

Other: I'd like to say a rather brief word about other innovation, as I believe the most opportunity can be found in the rare cases where a project is truly innovative or original. There are a number of features or protocols on the spectrum of development that will be groundbreaking, and, as such, spotting these, accumulating them early and simply holding on provides a very real chance at a life-changing investment. To my knowledge, there is work being done on atomic swaps, trust-less staking, stablecoins and other exciting and original ideas, and I do my best to apply the fundamental and technical analysis described in this book to point me in the direction of the most promising projects exhibiting these traits. When I do come across a rare project like this, I tend to accumulate a 1% bag, meaning a position that occupies 1% of the value of my entire altcoin portfolio, and I just hold on to it until the innovative development starts rolling out. There's little else to say on these, except that, if you find a project you feel is truly revolutionary in the space, don't hesitate and hold on tight.

Chapter Three

TECHNICAL ANALYSIS

Technical analysis; my preferred method of analysis, and the one that I rely most heavily on. Where fundamental analysis can be laborious, inconsistent and sometimes fruitless, technical analysis is formulaic and reliable. When I first joined the space, I recall thinking that technical analysis seemed like an impossible language to learn, but hundreds and hundreds of hours of studying later, I feel a strange fondness for it. Have I put you off? Yes, I really did have to spend a truly countless number of hours studying charts, in all their forms, in order to gain some level of understanding of them, and the most significant thing I learnt was to **keep it simple.** Too often do I see individuals posting charts on Twitter with thirty-six indicators and twelve criss-crossing diagonal trend-lines, bathed in the entire Pantone colour palette. In my experience, people overcompensate for a lack of understanding with cluttered charts. There are very few things you can put on chart of any real value, but those few things are invaluable.

In this chapter, I will run through the basic patterns and tools that I use, before elaborating on more specific concepts, such as price-action, orderbook reading and accumulation and distribution. Up first, patterns.

Chart Patterns

As I alluded to in the introductory passage of this chapter, the most consequential finding in my study of technical analysis was that the foundational principles one learns when they first approach the subject are the most dependable and beneficial of them all. Simplicity, in TA, is most conducive to profitable and efficient trading, and I would like to preface this section with a warning, of sorts, against the potential allure of indicators. They are unnecessary – and often ineffective – and are simply means of displaying price and volume data in different ways. Price and volume, therefore, are all one need worry about.

Now, I'm going to avoid the condescension of assuming you aren't aware of how price or volume are displayed on a chart, or what these terms mean, and instead run through the basic patterns that I look for, and the tools that I tend to utilise, before jumping into the bulk of what I study on a chart – price-action. I believe that having an understanding of traditional chart patterns is useful insofar as they allow one to adopt a retail mindset towards their analysis. By 'retail' I mean the majority of market participants: those of us who aren't trading for a bank or a fund. A retail mindset is the conventional approach to technical analysis that has been taught through books and seminars since its inception, and it relies heavily on traditional chart patterns and industry-standard indicators. It can be a successful approach, but, as with anything conventional in an industry in which 90% of participants are losers, it does not give a complete picture, and thus cannot be the most effective approach. The reason why, then, I believe that it is important to understand this approach is because one can glean from it the biases that affect the vast majority, as well as garner a fuller understanding of the market-maker, which we shall get into in the later sections. But first, the basics.

There are a vast number of traditional and non-traditional chart patterns that I could go into in this section, but, in truth, only a small number are all that useful for investing in altcoins. Many of the traditional patterns one can observe in the stock market do not tend to appear in altcoin markets but there are some that I like to keep an eye on.

Before we get into the actual patterns, there are a couple of things to clear up regarding the relationship between these patterns and trading altcoins: firstly, due to the low volume of many microcaps and lowcaps, often these patterns do not form, and, if they do, they are often undone by illiquid price-action (hence using a stop-loss for these is ineffectual). Where these patterns are drawn with greater frequency and consistency is in midcaps and highcaps, so keep that in mind if or when you attempt to utilise and exploit them. Secondly, I find these patterns more useful for shorter-term trading as opposed to the longer-term approach I have emphasised thus far in the book, but where they do become most informative for longer-term positions is in trade management. If, for example, a traditional pattern forms on a chart that is indicative of a bottom, and we have yet to fully accumulate the position that we have determined we would like to hold via our analysis, these patterns can be helpful in providing that extra push towards picking up the remainder of our position, lest the pattern completes and price breaks out, thus ridding us of that opportunity.

In several past trades, I have found myself deliberating the accumulation of a coin, having only picked up two-thirds or less of what I'd like to own, almost exclusively in expectation of lower, cheaper prices, and found, in the following days, traditional bottom patterns forming, such as an 'Adam and Eve'. Those are the cases in which I allow traditional patterns to influence my approach. And, speaking of an 'Adam and Eve', let's get stuck into the three patterns I do consider useful in the cryptosphere. Rest assured, I'll refrain from lengthy Investopedia-esque descriptions of the patterns and the like, all of which you could find for free online, and stick to the essentials for altcoin trading. Below the brief explanation of each, I have included an annotated example for further clarity on their usefulness.

Adam and Eve: The 'Adam and Eve' pattern is one of the most commonly observed in crypto, and is indicative of the formation of a bottom for price, usually followed by price growth.

Cup-and-Handle: The famous 'Cup-and-Handle' pattern is ever-present on crypto-Twitter, and is actually one of the more reliable patterns to utilise, in my experience. It's incredibly easy to spot because of how distinct it is, and I tend to find them forming most commonly on the more-established coins with higher volume. The pattern is another that is indicative of a bottom, often followed by price breakouts on volume to signal reversals.

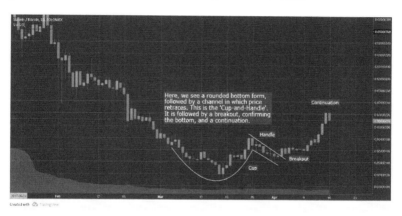

Head-and-Shoulders: When I was trading forex, 'Head-and-Shoulders' patterns were my favourite to look out for. I did find them rather effective prior to transitioning my technical analysis approach to focus on price-action. However, you don't often see them forming in altcoins, especially not in microcaps or lowcaps, and the inverted form of the pattern is the only one I pay attention to when it does form, because it can be indicative of a bottom. One thing I continue to like about this pattern is that it can form within a fairly narrow accumulation channel, and thus can be used as a genuine signal for buying.

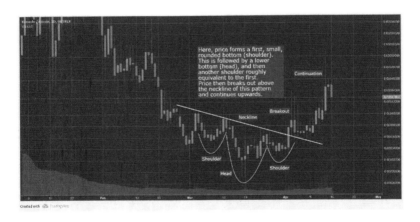

Those really are the only three patterns I implement in my trading strategy, though they do not play an active role in my analysis. However, spend some time scouting these patterns out, simply to train your eye for them – by making yourself familiar with these patterns, you can see what the majority are anticipating when they look at a chart, and that puts you a step ahead. If you don't need to remain on standby for the possible formation of a pattern prior to taking some action, you are closer aligned with smart-money. Smart-money doesn't wait for an 'Adam and Eve' pattern prior to accumulating a new position – they anticipate and precede its formation (or the formation of all other patterns) and buy far earlier. How can we know, then, when the best time is to begin buying any given coin? I hope that the following sections of this chapter will help to illuminate that.

Price-Action

What is price-action? Price-action is an approach to technical analysis in which everything on a chart is ignored except the price and volume data, and my approach has been heavily influenced by a trader that goes by the pseudonym, *InnerCircleTrader*, or ICT. As I mentioned in the first half of the book, stumbling upon ICT changed my outlook on technical analysis almost entirely, and I have since continued to use his concepts and teachings in much of my analysis in crypto. Since I am not ICT, I won't be teaching his concepts in this section (though I will include a couple of crypto-related examples of his concepts to show how effectively they work), but I highly recommend anyone wanting a comprehensive knowledge of all there is to know about price-action analysis to seek out whatever material you can by him.

For reference, his website is http://www.theinnercircletrader.com/.

However, there is much within price-action that is common knowledge to those who study it, and many of the most fundamental principles of technical analysis, such as horizontal support and resistance, fall under it. If I told you that the vast majority of the accumulation and distribution of my positions was reliant upon straight lines on a chart, would you believe me? Well, it most certainly is. Rarely do I find myself pissing about with much else on a chart besides horizontal support and resistance anymore, with a couple of trend-lines and the odd Fibonacci retracement thrown in for good measure (the only non-price-derived tool that I use).

There are a few key price-action concepts that I pay attention to, and these are as follows: horizontal support and resistance; trend-lines; orderblocks (an ICT concept); Fibonacci retracements and extensions; and volume. Mastering those five tools will provide you with all you need to successfully implement technical analysis within your trading strategy. Let's crack on.

Support and Resistance: This is the bedrock of all TA. It is the first means of analysis that most learn when beginning their journeys and the most effective means that they will ever encounter. Support is simply an area where an influx of buyers is expected to *support* price. Resistance is an area where an influx of sellers is expected to force price downwards. These concepts can be simplified further: they are, in part, the manifestation of supply and demand on a chart. Areas of strong support will be difficult for price to break below, and areas of strong resistance will be difficult for price to break above. Thus, buying at support and selling at resistance becomes a foundational lesson of technical analysis. To direct this more towards altcoin markets, consider the pace at which we experience growth and depreciation in the cryptosphere. The markets are furiously fast in their movement, and so, unlike in traditional markets, price does not take years to find long-term support and resistance levels. Instead, these levels are found relatively often. How is this useful for us? Well, given that we are focusing our attention on longer-term positions that offer the opportunity for exponential growth with limited downside risk, these opportunities become much more frequent when the market cycle – that is, the movement between periods of growth to periods of depreciation – completes so rapidly.

But how does one exploit these levels? My approach is very straightforward and takes place exclusively on the daily time-frame. Below, I've written up a step-by-step breakdown of how I identify these levels on a chart:

1. Firstly, load up your browser and navigate to a charting platform, such as TradingView or Coinigy.

2. Once you've found an altcoin you want to chart (for this example, I'm using LibraryCredits), begin by selecting the horizontal line tool from the toolbar. Make sure the chart is on the daily time-frame.

3. Place a horizontal line above every major swing-high and below every major swing-low. A swing-high is a pattern comprised of three or more candles, in which the middle candle forms a peak in price. A swing-low is where the middle candles forms a trough in price. These are both displayed in the image on the following page. Make sure to include the wicks of the candles.

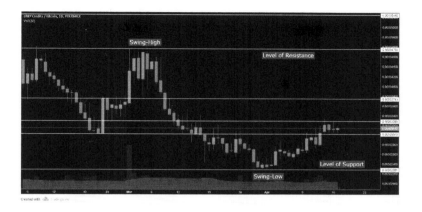

4. Each horizontal line above a swing-high is a level of
    resistance: price failed to continue beyond this
    point, and thus it will be a significant level in the
    future. Each horizontal line below a swing-low is a
    level of support: price refused to descend below this
    point. Observe how price has reacted previously at
    these levels; how they draw price in towards them
    like magnets. Because we are doing this exercise on
    the daily time-frame, these levels become all the
    more significant than if we were to repeat it on the
    hourly chart. These are long-term support and
    resistance levels – exactly what we require to
    evaluate the accumulation and distribution of
    positions.

5. Now, using the horizontal lines you have plotted,
    determine where, if at all, support or resistance
    levels switch roles and become their counterpart. In
    short, where does support become resistance, and

resistance become support? These price levels are particularly significant, as we can observe by the higher level of activity around them. Any level where price is continually switching between a point of support and a point of resistance is one to pay particular attention to in the future. Using the above chart again, I have depicted this for clarity in the image below.

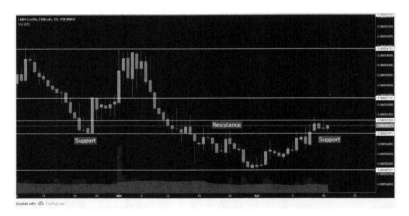

6. Repeat this on every altcoin chart for an entire exchange. Seriously, do it.

That's the entirety of my approach to horizontal support and resistance. Simple, isn't it? When you finish up with plotting out all these levels on a hundred or more altcoin charts, you'll realise just how powerful such a straightforward method can be. Time and time again, these price levels are respected, and the more familiar you get with them, the more effectively you'll be able to exploit them. We'll return to these levels in the *Accumulation and Distribution* section, but, for now, onto trend-lines.

Trend-lines: In truth, I have had a rocky relationship with trend-lines. During the time I spent poring over material on TA, conflicting resources would tell me that 'trend-lines are useless' and 'trend-lines are paramount.' What I've found – as with most things – is that the truth is somewhere in the middle. I have recently returned to inclusion of trend-lines in my TA, as I have witnessed how helpful they can be when combined with other tools.

A trend-line is just diagonal support or resistance. As can be observed in the image that follows, trend-lines can repress or uphold price for extended periods of time, and thus they must be monitored to have a more complete understanding of why price is acting in the way it is.

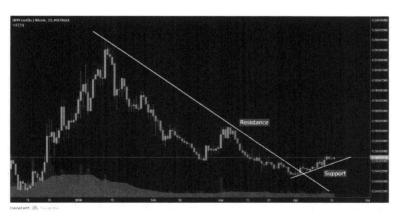

Now, contrary to conventional wisdom, I buy whilst price is below the resistance trend-line, in anticipation of a breakout. The traditional approach is to await a breakout above the line and buy when price retests it. This is all well and good if you're a short-term trader, looking for double-digit percentage gains, but we want minimal downside risk with maximum upside potential. After price has broken out above the resistance trend-line, upside potential is decreasing whilst downside risk is increasing. If our buys precede a breakout, we can get the best possible entry. But how do we determine where below trend to begin buying? The opportunity to minimise downside risk and maximise upside potential is lost if one buys too early... and this is where combining trend-lines with horizontal support and resistance comes into play.

Take a look at the chart on the following page. I have added a couple of long-term horizontal support and resistance levels – miraculously, they align with the range in which price reversed its long-term downtrend and broke out above it. This range of historical price-levels gives us a strong indication as to where this reversal might occur, as the last time price reached those levels it found support and rallied.

Now, check out the following chart, which depicts a twelve-month period of price-history.

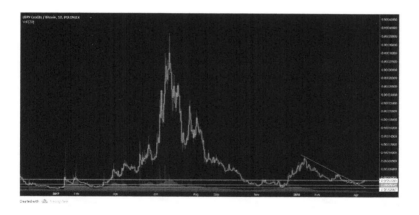

I haven't altered the horizontal support and resistance lines from the previous chart, yet observe how these levels remain significant throughout the price-history of LibraryCredits. This is partly how I determine where below the trend I should begin buying. As you can see, a combination of horizontal and diagonal support and resistance is essential if you want to understand *why* price does what it does.

Volume: If price is principal, volume is second-in-command. Volume is a measure of the amount of trading activity that takes place within any given period, and, for this reason, it can provide some insight into the validity of price-action. By this, I mean that volume can confirm movements or deem them false. This becomes incredibly useful in the cryptosphere, what with the low-liquidity markets and the high levels of manipulation. Using volume, we can determine points of smart-money accumulation and distribution, as well as avoid the treachery of false breakouts.

Below, I've annotated a Dogecoin chart with these various points of analysis.

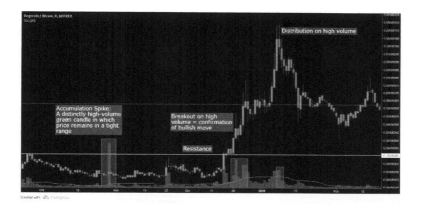

Let's go through this point-by-point:

Firstly, volume is invaluable for spotting when and where market-makers might be accumulating a position. Look at the first volume bar I have highlighted on the chart – notice how it exceeds all of the other volume bars. This shows that this one single day had more volume than any other in the time-period displayed on the chart, and the fact it is a green candle (though that won't be apparent given the black-and-white image) indicates that this was a bullish day. However, when we look at the price candle itself, we can see that very little movement occurred whatsoever – price remained within a tight range despite the market experiencing an outstanding amount of volume. What this suggests is that some market participant accumulated an extraordinarily large position within a very small price range, and we can safely assume that this is the work of a market-maker. In fact, there are a couple of moves we can make from here to further analyse this activity. The first move is to hover over the volume candle in question to find the actual amount of Dogecoin that was traded on that day. In this case, it is 14.24bn DOGE. Now, we make a simple calculation to work out the percentage this constitutes of the circulating supply of Dogecoin: 14.24bn / 111.7bn (on 29th October 2017) x 100 = 12.7%. Over a tenth of Dogecoin's circulating supply was traded in one 24-hour period. This is astronomical, especially for a top 50 market cap altcoin, and thus this is our first indicator that the market needs to be monitored. I make this calculation for all 'accumulation spike' candles (green volume candles that exceed all preceding or subsequent volume candles). The second move one can make is to combine this information with the aforementioned analysis of the rich-list, searching out where exactly this mass of Dogecoin had ended up.

But, I digress – back to volume itself. There is something that can be misleading about monitoring volume candles on a daily chart, and that is that, despite the candle closing green, the majority of the volume throughout the day may well have been from sellers, and a small flurry of price movement at the end of the day can cause these candles to close green, thus giving the impression that it was a day of dramatic accumulation. One way to counter this is to switch the time-frame to that of the four-hour or lower, and one can get a clearer picture of what exactly the daily volume is comprised of.

Below, there is a four-hour Dogecoin chart, depicting the exact same periods of volume that I highlighted on the original chart. Closer inspection confirms our hypothesis that the twenty-four-hour period in question experienced an abnormal amount of buying. One can place volume under greater scrutiny by continuing to move down through the time-frames to pinpoint this price-action more exactly, if one so wishes, but I tend to just stick to the four-hour and perhaps the hourly charts for confirmation of my volume analysis.

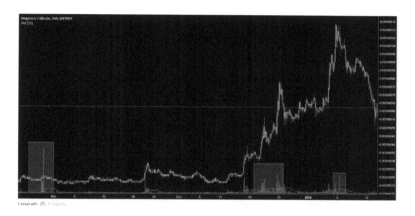

Returning to the first Dogecoin chart, the next use-case for volume comes when price breaks out of a range it was previously contained within. Observe the line of resistance that holds price down for an extended period – notice how, when price breaks above this line, it is accompanied by a large increase in volume. What this tells us is that this movement is authentic. If the break above resistance occurred with little to no volume, it would imply that the likelihood is that the breakout is a false one, intended to lead the sheep to slaughter by inviting a flurry of retail buying.

The third use-case for volume is in spotting distribution. This is simply the reverse of what I referred to in the previous paragraphs on accumulation. Distinctly large red volume candles can be indicative of smart-money offloading their positions, and should be monitored in the same manner as their counterparts.

Fibonacci: Whilst not strictly a price-action tool, Fibonacci retracements and extensions are integral to my technical analysis approach, and, when employed in conjunction with support and resistance and volume, they are highly effective.

A Fibonacci retracement is a tool used to predict the pull-back of price after a period of growth based on a set of predetermined percentages, most commonly: 23.6%; 38.2%; 50%; 61.8%; and 78.6%. The figures used are often either there or thereabouts. A Fibonacci extension is used to find targets for growth after a pull-back. For extensions, the only figures I use are the 161.8% extension and the 200% extension, and so on and so forth through each century of percentages. The idea is that price will be drawn to the levels that are generated by these numbers – which, in turn, are drawn from ratios found within the sequence of Fibonacci numbers – and they form support and resistance in and of themselves. In my experience, they have worked a charm, though some individuals consider them a kind of woo-woo akin to indicators, and that's fair enough. If they aren't working for you, it makes sense not to include them in your strategy.

There does seem, however, to be some confusion as to how exactly these tools should be used, and many traders refuse to learn them out of fear at how complicated they can seem on the surface. The truth could not be further apart, and Fibonacci retracements and extensions can be the most simple of tools to implement in your trading. People just like to overcomplicate everything.

As for their use-cases within my altcoin trading strategy, extensions are more useful than retracements, as, in general, I'm not looking to add to positions on the way up. However, they are very useful if one *is* looking to do that, plus they can provide good entry levels if one has missed out on the accumulation range for a coin and is still keen on holding a position. Extensions play a larger part in my strategy than retracements as they are involved in the distribution process. I use the levels presented by the extensions and look for confluence with historical support and resistance levels, and these levels then become sell targets for my positions.

So, how does one go about drawing a Fibonacci retracement or extension? The method is very straightforward, but I've included an image of each on the following pages.

For a retracement, you simply take your Fibonacci tool on your charting platform and place it at the lowest price of a major swing-low (remember, we talked about what these are in the *Support and Resistance* section). Now, drag the tool all the way up to the highest price of a major swing-high. The tool will be preset with the most common figures, but you can tinker with this in the settings – I tend to primarily use the 61.8% and 78.6% retracements. What you will find is a series of price-levels appear at these retracement percentages. It's that simple.

For an extension, you want to do the reverse of this: drop the tool on the highest price of a major swing-high and drag it down to the lowest price of a major swing-low. On TradingView, the 161.8% extension will be preset, but on other charting platforms you may need to configure this yourself. Configure whichever other extension levels you would like to appear (as I say, I like to use the 161.8%, 200%, 261.8% and 300%, and so forth). And voila, your required extension levels will appear.

Below is an image of a Fibonacci retracement on the Synereo (AMP) chart.

And here is an image of a Fibonacci extension. The major swing-high is the peak of the range and the major swing-low is its trough. Using these two points, we can map out potential levels at which the growth of AMP might be capped, and it stops around the 361.8% extension.

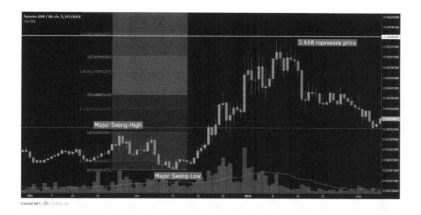

That draws this section to a close, and fear not, we'll get into how these levels are implemented in the strategy in the *Accumulation and Distribution* section.

Orderblock Examples: Now, I did mention orderblocks in the introductory passage of this chapter, and I once again implore you to seek out material by ICT if you want to learn about them, but I think it'll help exhibit the effectiveness of the material if I show you a few examples of orderblocks in altcoin markets. Before that, a brief explanation of what an orderblock *is* is required: an orderblock is the buy or sell candle that immediately precedes a major price move the opposite way. Thus, a bearish orderblock is the green candle that precedes a descent, and a bullish orderblock is the red candle that precedes an ascent. That is an incredibly simplified description but it will suffice for the purposes of the following examples.

Over the following pages, there are printed three examples of the effectiveness of both bullish and bearish orderblocks in crypto. If you find them compelling, get studying that material.

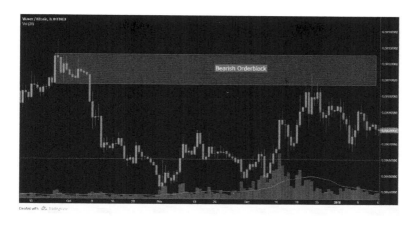

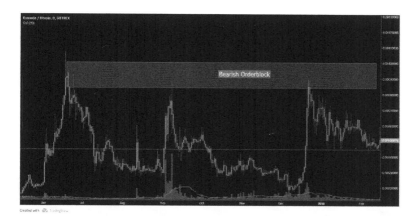

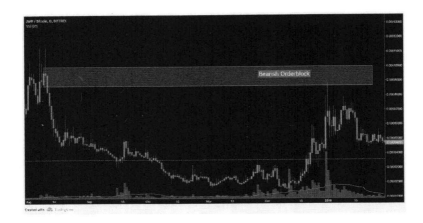

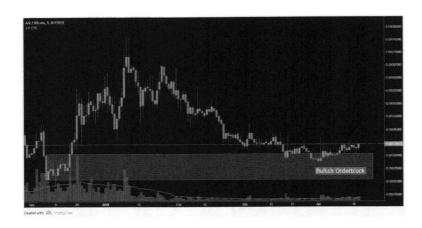

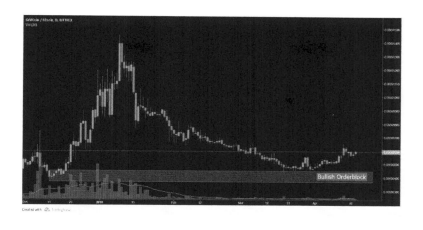

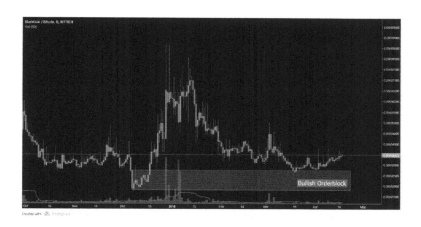

179

Fractals and Projection

This is a fun topic to consider, and one that much of has little basis in empirical evidence, and, rather, relies on experience for its authority. Nonetheless, projection, as I like to call it, is an interesting way to look at charts, and fractals are even more fascinating. A fractal – in the context of charting – is just a pattern of price-action that repeats on different scales throughout price-history. We see these fractals appearing all over the place, not just in the world of trading. What is important to remember is that a fractal is by no means a sure thing – just because price looks to be repeating a historical pattern, doesn't mean that it will continue to. What fractals do is allow us to see how price could be moving based on how it has moved before, and this is useful insofar as that it gives us a greater familiarity with the markets we are speculating on. Furthermore, spotting a fractal that supports one's analysis can offer a feeling of reassurance about one's positions. It's an incredibly fascinating thing to be looking for, and watching fractals play out perfectly post-observation is both satisfying and informative. The hard truth of the concept is that it is ultimately down to experience as to how acutely one can identify them, but I will do my best to illuminate their presence in altcoin markets in this section.

Consider this chart for Neutron:

What is readily observable from that chart is the pattern by which price repeats, even as intimately as to form a double top in the third box of each cycle, just on a different scale. There really is very little by way of information that I can offer to aid in you being able to pick up these price patterns except to suggest that, whilst completing the exercises set in this chapter, you spend a great deal of time poring over these charts and really **looking** at them. What that Neutron chart taught me when I first observed the fractal was that the fourth box of the cycle was likely to provide the optimal time and price for entry, given that the following box would likely be a period of explosive growth.

A more practical approach to this line of thinking – namely, pattern recognition – is something I call projection, though I'm sure there must be a legitimate name for the technique, and it is simply the act of measuring the market cycles, or its constituent parts, and considering them as potential fractals. More plainly put, we take the lowest price on a chart (a trough) and measure the number of days between it and the highest price on the chart (a peak): this is its bull cycle – the period in which price grows from its lowest to its highest. We then measure the number of days between that same peak and the subsequent trough: this is its bear cycle. The sum of these is the number of days price took to complete one full market cycle. Another measure we take is peak-to-peak, though, naturally, this is only applicable for coins with an established price-history. Using these date ranges, we can project them forward, making the assumption that the market-maker will adhere to a similar, if not identical, timescale between the market cycles.

Consider Linx:

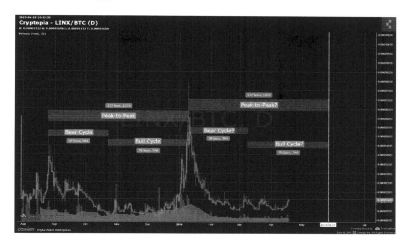

I have marked out the date ranges on the chart above (you can do this using the date range tool on TradingView or Coinigy). If we project the first cycle forward, though not identical, the ranges are similar, with price now looking as though it is attempting a breakout to begin its ascent towards a peak in the end of May. What I find useful about applying this technique to my charts is that it gives them a structure of sorts, and provides a different perspective on the habits of the market-maker, and thus of price. It almost maps out a potential trajectory for price that is independent of any other form of analysis.

Apply this approach to as many of your charts as you can, and you will find an abundance of markets that have little to no pattern to their price-action at all, but some that operate near-identically every cycle. If they operate so repetitively at such a high frequency (three cycles of similar behaviour or more), the balance of probability suggests that the likelihood is this pattern will continue to repeat itself, and that can provide a world of comfort during periods of accumulation.

Below, I've included a couple of charts to demonstrate this: one of NXT, and one of Dogecoin.

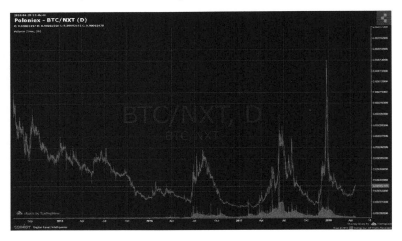

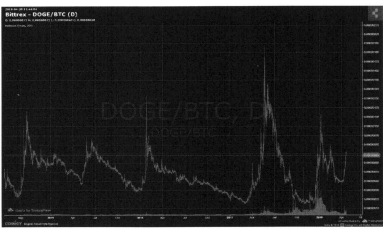

These charts need not even be annotated to identify the overt pattern of their price-action. Using the principles of fractals and projection alone – and given a sufficient time-frame to work with – we can see how these peaks and troughs reoccur at similar price-levels and within similar durations. Sure, one cycle might be more extended than the previous one or indeed shorter, but the fundamental structure of each cycle remains largely the same. Now, imagine we combined this with the various methods of fundamental and technical analysis available to us – the confidence one can have in buying those troughs time and time again becomes immense.

I stress, however, that this is not an approach that should be used exclusively, but rather is most useful when used in conjunction with all other means of analysis. Regardless, it is another tool for the toolbox.

Orderbook Reading

If I had to choose one trading technique or tool that provided me with the most utility throughout my time involved in altcoin speculation, I would have to give that title to orderbook reading. I owe the success I found in 2014 almost entirely to this method of analysis, and it remains, to this day, the sole piece of knowledge that I discovered myself – no Google, no YouTube tutorials, nothing except my own hours of research. In truth, I attribute much of my shaping as a speculator to the period in which I first learnt to examine an orderbook.

Before I dive into the method and other details, and, as this section comes with no substantial introduction, I think it may be helpful to briefly outline what I mean by 'reading' an orderbook. The orderbook is simply the ledger of orders on any given market, on any given exchange, and comprises of a number of asks and bids, or buys and sells. You can find orderbooks for almost all tradeable assets, though their utility is either negligible or for entirely different purposes outside of the cryptosphere. At first, I had little knowledge whatsoever on how an orderbook could be used for anything other than finding the orders required to execute the trades you wanted. And, to many, that is all an orderbook is. But what this ledger provides is information on the possible present and future intent of market-makers. The reason why I believe orderbook reading is so useful in crypto specifically is because the industry is still in its infancy, and so, market volume for individual altcoins is minimal, relative to other tradeable assets. Because of this, much more can be garnered from where and what orders are placed than in any of those other markets. The market-makers are made visible, to a degree. And that slight degree of visibility gives us an edge, if you know how to exploit it.

Back in 2014, when I first began actively trading, I was unaware of orderbook reading as a method of analysis, with little to no information available in the obvious places – traditional technical analysis websites and books do not reference it – and I knew that I needed to figure out a way to kerb the losses and learn to be one step ahead of the rest of the pack; become the 10% as opposed to the 90. Traditional TA was helpful, for sure, but I was still losing in those early days, and I had not yet discovered the wonderful world of price-action, and, as a voracious teenager, determined to learn and find success, research and information was my way in.

There was an abundance of novel information, since this was an industry in its infancy, but there was not much on where and what to research. I figured out relatively early that the orderbooks I thought were only useful for executing orders actually displayed much more than appeared on the surface. Pattern-recognition is a marvellous thing. I began to notice similarities – more significantly, recognise legitimate patterns – between orders within any single coin pair, and between orders across markets. The more time I spent monitoring the orderbooks, the more readily I could trace the similarities. I probably spent the best part of a hundred hours before I had grown some sense of familiarity with the orderbook, with much of that time being spent quite literally staring at single orders: where they were placed; when they were placed; how often they were removed and replaced; the order sizes; the order patterns etc.

But what exactly did I learn? I will detail the entirety of my knowledge as concisely as one can afford to when dealing with a subtle, often elusive technique such as this. One thing I would like to add prior to this is that this information was certainly a little more easy to apply in 2014/15 than it currently is: with Bittrex's orderbook display now limited to ten pages, and the later pages seemingly useless (more on that later), some coin pairings are harder to read now than they used to be. Poloniex is still a useful exchange for orderbooks, as is Cryptopia, but the lower-volume exchanges can be difficult to read, and more challenging than they are often worth. Regardless, this information will still prove useful, as it does for my own speculation to this day.

The Method:

The one thing that cannot be imparted via books or tutorials is patience, and that is an essential trait to possess if you want to use orderbooks to their full advantage. But, if you believe you have the level of patience necessary, then grab a notebook and open up a few tabs on your browser with each of your favourite exchanges. To begin to familiarise yourself with what an orderbook can provide, you need to know what it is that differentiates it from many other tools of analysis: namely, the fact that the orderbook reveals details about **potential** price movement. Repeat that to yourself until it clicks. It is a very simple fact, but one that is so often overlooked and neglected by traders. Why is it that these details appear in orderbooks and not elsewhere in analysis? It is because market-makers cannot just 'paint' future prices onto a chart, nor can they move price without orders. The orderbook is the very first point-of-contact for price-action.

There is an exercise I formulated back when I was discovering this that allowed me to develop my pattern-recognition skills:

1. Pick out three to five coin pairs. Any will do, but the most useful for the exercise are midcaps that feature on several exchanges. For example: UBQ/BTC, LBC/BTC, VIA/BTC.

2. For each of those pairs, note down the top two exchanges for volume, respectively. For example: UBQ/BTC: 1. Bittrex 2. Cryptopia.

3. Now for the taxing part: spend as much time as you can every day noting down some important details for each coin pair on both exchanges. You will need to go through as much of the orderbook as time allows you, and note: the time of note-taking; the total bid/buy volume of orders on each exchange; the total ask/sell volume of orders on each exchange; the 10 largest buy orders (at what price they are placed, their sizes in BTC, their quantities in the given coin); the 10 largest sell orders (same details as the buys).

4. Do this for a week, and make sure you record in as much detail as you can. You may do the exercise during the same time period each day, or a different period each day, it doesn't matter as long as you note it down. Remember, you are developing pattern-recognition, and sometimes that isn't in the form of the orders themselves but the *time* you read the orderbook. Market-makers constantly manipulate orderbooks, pulling and placing orders at all hours – what we are watching for is similarities, patterns and mistakes.

5. By the end of the week, you should be mentally drained by the time spent poring over orderbooks. Ideally, you should at least be beginning to notice patterns and recognise details without needing to write everything down, though this takes a lot longer than a week before it embeds itself in your brain.

Even at this point, with all of the information you have noted down over the seven days, you are already steps ahead of the vast majority of the traders in crypto. But how are the details relevant, and how can they help you to pick out a winner? The answer to that is extensive, depending on one's trading proclivity, with some details being extremely useful for short-term trades and others more helpful to the long game. The point is that all of the information you need to figure out how a coin's price is being manipulated and where it may be headed in the future is in that notebook now. For the sake of brevity, I will forego any further preamble and get to the specifics of what you should be looking for within these details. I'll begin with the simpler details before moving onto the more advanced stuff:

Order depth: Though it can be rare to find, what you should be looking for is a bid/buy side that is thicker and heavier than the ask/sell side of the orderbook. Usually, what you will find is the opposite, since the primary purpose of trading altcoins for many people, myself included, is to increase the value of my portfolio in BTC, not any other cryptocurrency, and so, traders are more often looking for the exit than the entry. Furthermore, what you may find is that the surface-level buy depth is larger than the sell depth. What I mean by surface-level is that, of the orders within a given percentage of the current price, there are more buy orders than sell orders; and this is particularly true on Bittrex, where the default order depth viewable is not the entirety of the orderbook. This is far more common than finding the same to be true of the entire orderbook. However, do not dismiss this, as it *can* be an indicator for short-term demand, and thus, an incoming bullish move. I say 'can' because of the aforementioned manipulation ever-present in the orderbooks, which we will get into further into this section.

You can use order depth to supplement your analysis by using it to garner a market bias rather than a personal bias. What I mean by this is simply that a personal bias is discovered via analysis that is entirely subjective (for example, traditional technical analysis). The reason traditional TA is subjective is because it is only you drawing up that chart, placing on *your* patterns, *your* ideas for support and resistance and *your* favoured indicators. Order depth is not personal in this way because it provides information on what numerous interested parties think about any given coin, hence a sort of 'market bias' can be discovered. The general rule that I use – having already discounted the manipulation patterns that I will share later – is that a bid side valued at a higher total amount of BTC than the ask side is often a diamond in the rough, due to the rare occurrence of such order depth.

I asked you to note down what the total values of both sides of the orderbook were, in the given coin as well as in bitcoin, for the instances that this information is available. This is significant for the next kind of order depth: namely, that the bid side is equal to or higher in, for example, the total amount of UBQ than the ask side. This information is provided on Bittrex for all coin pairs, and is useful in shedding light on the quality of the orders themselves.

To make this clearer, imagine UBQ/BTC on Bittrex has 20BTC of total buy support, and the total buy support in UBQ is 133,333.333 – this gives an average buy order value of 0.00015BTC per UBQ, which is pretty solid given its current value, and suggests that market participants are generally willing to pay a fair price for their UBQ. Now imagine that the total buy support is still 20BTC, but the total buy support in UBQ is 1,500,000 – this scenario gives an average buy order value of 0.00001333BTC per UBQ. 1333 satoshis is pittance, given the current price, and suggests that the average market participant is less willing to pay current prices for their UBQ, and that price may move lower to accommodate.

Of course, averages are temperamental, and by no means give us certainty on price-action, but this is important information to consider. Where this gets tricky is on the ask side of the orderbook, as many exchanges do not provide BTC totals for it. As far as I can remember, only Bittrex offer this information without need for a little extra digging, and so, sell order averages can be discovered readily on their markets, but for most other exchanges you will need to put in the effort in unearthing this information. It isn't difficult work, but it can be tiresome. In short, you would simply note down the total volume of sell orders in the given coin, and then scroll down or through the ask side of the orderbook to find out the total BTC amount, as many exchanges provide a running total for this alongside the orders. From there, the information can be used in the same way as the bid order depth.

For example, using UBQ/BTC again, let us say that there are 1000BTC of sells placed, equating to 5,000,000 UBQ – this would give an average sell order value of 0.0002BTC per UBQ, which is only 25-30% above where it currently resides, suggesting that most market participants aren't expecting much of an increase in price prior to finding their exits. However, if there was a total of 2500BTC of sells placed, equating to 1,000,000 UBQ, our average sell order value moves up to 0.0025BTC per UBQ, suggesting that very few are willing to sell their UBQ anywhere close to current prices.

Take all of this order average analysis with a pinch of salt, however, as, not only can values be skewed by spoof orders and manipulation, but they can be far lower and far higher for buy and sell order averages, respectively, than other analysis would deem reasonable. For example, the current bid side of UBQ on Bittrex gives an average order value of 0.000025BTC, roughly, and, given all other factors of analysis, the likelihood of price reaching this level is slim. How this information becomes useful in these cases is that it gives us an indication of willingness to sell or to buy at any given level, and, when coupled with distribution/rich-list analysis, can suggest where market-makers would like to take price in the future.

Time: Time is a tricky detail to analyse, often proving more time-consuming than the findings themselves are worth. What I will say, however, is that it is indispensable for discovering market manipulation, and, though this section will be shorter than the last, it is no less significant for those wanting to suss out the habits of their coin's puppet master. And make no mistake about it, almost every coin in existence will have somebody pulling the strings of its price-action.

The details I asked you to note down allow you to figure out a number of important aspects to the manipulation of any given coin: namely, whether or not there may *be* much orderbook manipulation; the lifestyle habits of a market-maker; whether there is more than one market-maker; and which orders are most likely spoof orders. I will sequentially run through how each of these nuggets of information can be discovered using time.

To begin, you will need to have watched the orderbooks of any given coin pair on any given exchange religiously. This is the only way to exploit time for analysis, as there are actions that take place at all hours. Also, I would like to make clear that, of all orderbook analysis, time is the most precarious, and it works most successfully on coins that are not highcaps and with lower circulating supply. The reason for this being that lower coin supply leads to a freer orderbook, as we established earlier in the book. Highcap coins with high supply – for example, Siacoin – would be extremely challenging to use time analysis on because the prices are low in satoshi-denomination, and, as such, the orderbook is too tight and heavy to ascertain whether any given order is actually multiple market participants or just one.

Firstly, to discover whether the coin pair is truly being manipulated, and the level at which this is taking place, (though there are other, more certain methods by which to come to such a conclusion), simply note down the largest buy and sell orders within 50% of the current price of the coin, including the time at which you viewed these orders. Return to the orderbook twelve hours later, and do exactly the same thing. Are all the orders exactly the same as there were? Have some changed, or been removed entirely? Keep doing this every twelve hours for a week and noting down changes, if any, as well as a lack of any change. If you return to the orderbook every time to find that the orders you initially noted down have not changed at all, the likelihood is that orderbook manipulation is not taking place at this price-level, but I don't think I have ever really found such a scenario.

Altcoins have extremely dynamic markets, and the more likely case is that you do indeed find some changes. If you return to find that some of the larger orders have been removed, this implies two possibilities: firstly, that the market-maker for this coin is asleep or away during this time-period, and thus, you have discovered some information about their habits, and secondly, if this is true, then those removed orders are most likely spoof orders, used to move price one way or another, or to hold it in place, but never intended to be filled. As I mentioned, time is challenging to examine, and in order to garner the most from it, you have to continually check these details and establish a pattern. Perhaps they are based in Europe and pull their spoof orders around midnight GMT, and perhaps these orders return at 7am GMT, ready for the new trading day. Establishing these kinds of patterns gets you closer to the market-maker, and understanding the entity behind the movements in price is invaluable.

However, there is another scenario that is also common: the largest buy or sell orders within 50% of the current price are removed twelve hours after you initially spot them, and replaced by orders of different weight at different prices. What this suggests, in my opinion, is that there are two or more market-makers playing the coin pair, manipulating price within differing time-zones. Whilst I will get into more detail about actual order values and prices in the next section, and what they can express, I will state that, in the above scenario, the way to figure out if it is true that there are multiple market-makers at work is to recognise the patterns of order placement. Different market-makers favour different styles of order placement, and spotting this, coupled with spotting that significant orders are removed and replaced intermittently during different time-zones, is one way of being certain. Turns out this section wasn't that much shorter...

Order Patterns: The most useful information that can be gathered from an orderbook is the *pattern* of order placement, order value and order depth. This comprises of a vast number of details to keep an eye on, including buy walls, sell walls, clean orders and other forms of orders. Pattern-recognition is the ultimate means by which to utilise the resources available in an orderbook, as it not only provides concrete data on present price-action, but allows for predictions to be made on future movements. There is a great deal to look out for, and this is the most advanced stage of orderbook reading, but all of this will become more readily identifiable with experience.

The most simple form of pattern-recognition here is the concept of a clean order. What I mean by a 'clean order' is one that exhibits the most effortless and comprehensible numerical values. The most obvious examples of this are orders comprising of multiples of 5 or 10, such as a bid of 10000 UBQ at 0.00015BTC, or an ask of 5000 UBQ at 0.0002BTC. These are both clean orders, so to speak. Often, these kinds of orders will be spread throughout the orderbook, indicating significant price-levels. You may see something to the effect of 10 orders of exactly 5000 UBQ in the sell-side, with each order placed at 5000-satoshi intervals. This is a pattern that is easy to recognise, and almost always is a footprint that the market-maker is forced to leave behind when manipulating price. What's more, it is a footprint that literally displays the blueprint for a potential pump. Very rarely does one find such an orderbook that is not the work of a market-maker laying the groundwork for a future pump. How can this information help you, as a speculator? Well, aside from the obvious value that one gets out of getting to know your maker, or, in this case, market-maker, you can use these orders to structure your own trades; use the given framework as the skeleton upon which your positions are fleshed out. Use the clean orders to find confluence with your own technical targets, for example.

This concept also translates to order value in bitcoin-denomination, and is another way by which one can spot manipulation and the intentions of market-makers. The thing to look out for here is an order that totals to a clean, round number in bitcoin. For example: 12736 UBQ placed in a sell order at 0.00019629BTC gives a total order value of 2.5BTC, which is very clean, and the sure sign of a potential spoof order or suppression order. The reason this is a sure sign, in my opinion, is simple: how often does a regular market participant have a large position in a coin that totals to a clean amount of bitcoin at an arbitrary price? Not often. Of course, as with the entirety of this chapter, this is by no means a certainty, but merely a balance of probability. This entire skill is supplemented and guided by one's ability to discern probabilities from the information available.

Many traders, at least on Twitter, are seemingly aware of the concept of buy and sell 'walls' but what I often see is the opposite reaction to these trading phenomenon than what is logical. A wall is simply an order of great magnitude, often used to push and pull price. The extent of that magnitude is often dependent on the average trading volume and the market cap of a coin, though I have seen examples where 15BTC buy orders are set up on a coin that trades 2-3BTC per day. These orders can take the form of bids or asks, depending on the market-maker's intent, and generally direct 90% of traders (the losing majority) into their own demise.

For the inexperienced, the first sight of a wall can scare you into otherwise irrational action, forcing our trading to become emotional, and thus, unsuccessful. I completely understand why; when one logs onto Bittrex to find a 20BTC buy wall on any given market at the current price-level, one cannot help but feel a necessity to jump in for fear of losing out on what seems like the beginning of an upwards move – but please, **please**, just don't do it. Any time you have that urge, log out of the exchange, analyse your own emotions and assess why it would be a terrible idea to buy on a whim because of the appearance of a large buy order.

The reason why the emotional reaction is an irrational one is as follows: the purpose of a buy wall or a sell wall is to drive inexperienced market participants into the opposing orders, thus filling the orders required by market-makers to position themselves better. What often follows is a swift change in momentum – with a sell wall of equal or greater measure being placed and the buy wall being pulled, for example – and the inexperienced traders dumping their just-bought altcoin at a discount right into the jaws of the shark. The way to recognise whether a large order is a wall or truly an order waiting to be filled is to watch to see the frequency with which the order is changed or removed. A wall tends to get pulled and shifted around very frequently, whereas true orders remain in the orderbook indefinitely. Also, sometimes you will see an order dumped into the buy wall, or bought from the sell wall, and these walls will subsequently get pulled. This is another means of identification. So, instead of playing the prey the next time you encounter walls, utilise your other methods of analysis and then, if all aligns, buy into a sell wall or exit into a buy wall. Play the market-maker, not vice-versa.

Bot orders are the next form of order that you need to learn to identify and take advantage of. The term is self-explanatory, but essentially what you are looking for is changes in the orderbook that defy human ability. For example, let us imagine you have just placed an order for 1000 UBQ at 0.00015BTC, and you occupy the top position in the bid side of the orderbook. No human can fill out and place an order above yours instantly after your own is placed. In these cases, you are witnessing a bot that is designed to do one of two things: either, it is attempting to push your order further up so that you purchase at a higher price, or it is trying to get as many fills as it possibly can, thus blocking other market participants from accumulating at this level. There is no easy way to tell which of the two it will be, other than to watch carefully and judge for yourself. I know that isn't a satisfactory resolution to the concept, but it is the only one I am aware of.

The final note of this section is on non-clean orders, or messy orders. These, by definition, are much more unclear and indistinguishable but work in exactly the same manner as clean order patterns. You are ultimately looking for the same thing: similarities in orders at important or regular intervals in the orderbook. By placing orders with awkward numerical values, market-makers are attempting to disguise their footprint. However, they are often lazy. Rather than placing several orders, each with an entirely different numerical value at arbitrary intervals, they must give themselves a recognisable framework, and so, what you will often find is 5 orders of 7327.8872501 UBQ at 1500-satoshi intervals, or something to that effect. When you find these identical but numerically-messy orders, make a note of them, as it is likely these are of significance and will be used to manipulate price in the same manner as the clean orders do.

This section ran on for far longer than I had initially planned it to, but I wanted to write extensively about this all since it is an important skill to develop. Regardless, I hope that it has been useful, and that you have gained some insight into a new way to approach the orderbook.

Accumulation and Distribution

Disregard market psychology and security and fundamental analysis and all of those other indirectly-related concepts for a brief moment: the two most important aspects directly related to trading are accumulation and distribution. That is, the buying of an altcoin, and the subsequent selling of that altcoin. Those are the two active mechanisms of a trade, and the only two things that can actually put money in your pocket (or portfolio). There are, undoubtedly, more important aspects of the trading process as a whole – for example, a poor approach to risk management will negate a good entry or exit – but it all boils down to the buy and the sell.

In this section, there are a couple of perspectives on accumulation and distribution that I'd like to cover: firstly, the identification of smart-money for both processes, and secondly, how these two processes take place in my own strategy. Since we covered a little on the former in the *Volume* section, I'll begin there. Plus, a comprehensive knowledge of how to spot when and where market-makers are buying or selling plays a part (or certainly should) in our own accumulation and distribution.

So, the elusive market-maker: how does one figure out where the so-called smart-money are buying into their positions, and, once they're in, how can we tell when they're getting out? The transparency of the cryptosphere makes this unquestionably more straightforward and accessible than in many other markets:

Smart-Money Accumulation: I believe there is a great deal of truth to the claim that the entry is the most important part of a trade, as a well-timed, cheap entry alleviates much of the risk. This is exactly why figuring out where smart-money is buying is worth the additional effort – what is the likelihood that the market participants responsible for the manipulation of price are going to buy their alts at prices that provide negative returns? Pretty much zero. They know where they want to buy, they know what they want their average prices to be, and they know where they want to run price up to when they have completed their accumulation. If we can track their footprints and follow the trail, we can realise a similar success rate in our own portfolios.

I will refrain from reiterating much of the material I've already covered on smart-money accumulation, such as volume spikes on charts and rich-list investigation, but, for the sake of clarity, I'll briefly mention them here before I get into other methods of analysis.

The volume data on a chart is critical in identifying the accumulation of a potential market-maker, as the appearance of green volume bars that exceed the other volume bars on the chart is indicative of large buying interest. Return to the *Volume* section earlier in this chapter for an elaboration on this. Rich-list investigation is equally critical, in that it can provide proof of accumulation by the top holders of any given coin, which can be cross-referenced with a chart to pinpoint the time and price at which the buying occurred. For further clarification, refer back to the *Block Explorers and Rich-Lists* section.

How else, then, can smart-money accumulation be detected? Well, as I began to describe earlier in the chapter, long-term horizontal support plays a big part in this. A plethora of seemingly wise quotes on the topic of trading are posted all over social media on a day-to-day basis; some are utter rubbish, but some are gold. One of these golden quotes is 'Buy when there's blood in the streets, *even if the blood is your own.*' This quote is often attributed to a Rothschild, though its origin is uncertain. Nonetheless, its point is incisive. Smart-money buys when things seem the worst, and sells when it all seems wonderful. And this is directly related to long-term support levels on a chart and their relationship to the market cycle, especially in crypto.

So, what exactly are we looking for? In short, we want to see tight price-ranges forming at long-term support after a market cycle has completed: this is where market-makers accumulate their positions for the next cycle (and this can be confirmed by cross-referencing with rich-lists), as it offers the greatest potential return with the smallest downside risk. The reason that these ranges often remain intact for many weeks is because it is a difficult and time-consuming process to accumulate a large position of an altcoin without significantly moving price. This is great for us, as it allows us the time to research potential positions comprehensively prior to entry. Anyway, I digress. Let's take a look at how this can be identified on charts.

Over the following pages, I have compiled a handful of annotated examples of smart-money accumulation:

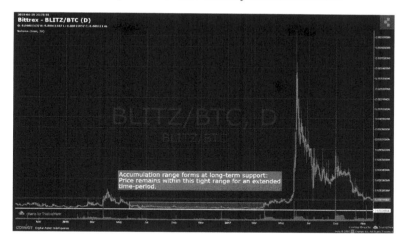

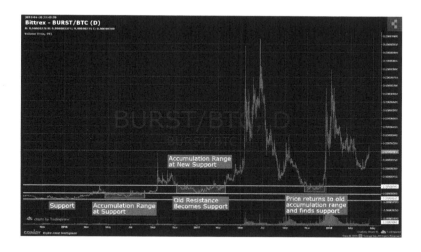

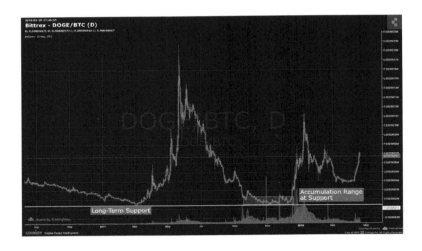

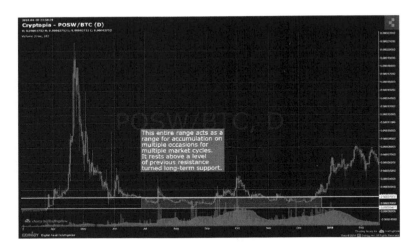

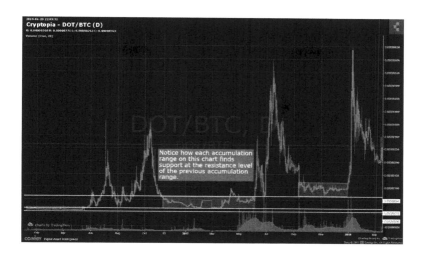

Notice how each accumulation range on this chart finds support at the resistance level of the previous accumulation range.

It is within these highlighted boxes that the vast majority of the smart-money accumulation occurs. Think about it: within these ranges, price is trading at levels of minimal historical downside risk and maximum upside potential, and it has completed a full market cycle, having descended from peaks to troughs, and thus majority sentiment is fearful. In other words, this is the optimal time to enter alts, and, given adequate fundamental and technical analysis of a coin itself – and evaluation of the assumed smart-money accumulation via volume and rich-list analysis – these ranges should provide all the time and confidence required to position yourself for the subsequent market cycle.

Now, that's all well and good, but when should you exit?

Smart-Money Distribution: Thankfully, much of what needs to be said on the topic of smart-money distribution has already been explained in the previous section – this is merely the reverse process. There is still, of course, much to clarify. By this, I mean that the process of identifying distribution is very much similar to that of accumulation:

Firstly, regarding rich-list analysis, one need only monitor the top addresses for negative changes in their balances **at the peaks of these market cycles**, as I explained in the *Block Explorers and Rich-Lists* section. As for volume-based analysis, we are looking for distinctly-large red volume candles after price growth, of which I provided examples of in the *Volume* section. But how can we anticipate where smart-money distribution may occur, so that our analysis can be most effective? Well, glance back at the charts from the previous pages – notice how swiftly price reverses at peaks, relative to the elongated periods of accumulation. Distribution unfolds at a faster pace than its counterpart, and, as such, we must act far faster in our exits than in our entries. Or must we? Given sufficient forward-planning and analysis of price-history, we can exit partially all the way to the peak, not fearing about catching or missing the ultimate top. And this is the approach I take with all of my trades. One can never know where the exact top will form, and given the violent and accelerated nature of a reversal from bull-cycle to bear-cycle, it's better to be cautious and prepared.

A strategy of partial distribution of a position at predetermined price-levels is, in my opinion, the most effective method of realising the greatest gains whilst diminishing risk on the way up. A great entry is no good if you hold all the way to the peak and back down to the lows again. Given that we can't predict tops as accurately as we can bottoms in altcoin markets, the next-best thing is to figure out where smart-money might be looking to distribute. Now, remember that market-makers have large positions – positions that cannot be exited all at once at the peak of the cycle, despite the large red volume candles you will spot around those areas. That is a significant portion of the distribution, no doubt, but in the same way that smart-money buys blood, it sells ecstasy, and ecstasy can be felt all the way up to the top.

There are two tools that I use to identify potential price-levels for smart-money distribution:

1. I use historical horizontal resistance to map out previous peaks (if any) and other significant levels of prior distribution.

2. I use Fibonacci extensions to find targets beyond previous peaks.

Consider the DOT chart below, in which each previous cycle peak has been marked out as a level of prior resistance, and thus a potential distribution level for future cycles. Alongside these, each cycle has had a Fibonacci extension applied to it, drawn from the peak to the trough – the 161.8% extension has been a significant level in price-history, and thus would also be marked out as a potential level of smart-money distribution.

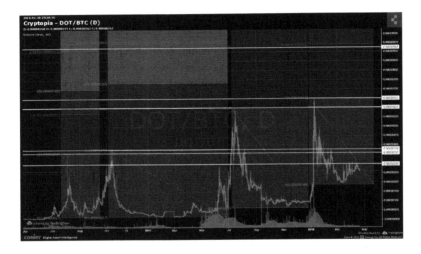

Once these potentially significant levels have been identified, rich-list and volume analysis is applied when price approaches them, and, if smart-money distribution is confirmed to be occurring, a predetermined portion of my position will also be sold at that level. This allows for partial selling to be feasible without requiring the position to be held indefinitely on an exchange, though it does mean that prices aren't always guaranteed, but I consider this a necessary risk given the far greater risk of unsecured funds.

To wrap this section up, there is sufficient transparency in the space to recognise when those that manipulate price are buying and when they are selling. Following their lead can only result in success.

Chapter Four

STAYING IN THE GAME

With the lengthier chapters now out of the way, we come to a couple of briefer but equally important ones, if not more so. Staying alive is the single hardest part of this game, especially when you're a newbie with little experience or knowledge of how to properly manage not only your portfolio but also risk itself. Couple this with an obliviousness to market psychology and market cycles, and an unfamiliarity with yourself as a speculator, and you have a recipe for near-instant disaster. Experience will alleviate many of these initial flaws, but I will do my best to accelerate that learning curve in the following sections on risk and portfolio management, and on market psychology.

Risk and Portfolio Management

This section may well be the most crucial in the entire book, especially in the context of speculating profitably, and what I have learnt over the previous few years is that a solid approach to risk and portfolio management is the single most effective way to create the most beneficial blend of minimised downside and maximised upside for your capital. Portfolio management is a far more straightforward topic, but relies a little on a comprehensive understanding of what risk is, and so, I will save elaboration on it until following the section on risk. Plus, in truth, portfolio management is more a calculated strategy than a philosophy, unlike my take on its counterpart.

Risk: Risk, in the context of speculation, can have multiple connotations. One definition of risk is that which is derived from the volatility of the underlying asset being traded: for example, a microcap is inherently more risky, in that a microcap suffers from greater and more erratic price swings, than a highcap. Furthermore, a microcap will undoubtedly suffer from weaker liquidity than a highcap, and this brings its own sense of risk. Another definition can be found in the context of one's portfolio, where 'risk' is the amount of capital one is willing to place in a position: for example, in a portfolio of 1 bitcoin, if one decided to invest 0.1BTC into an altcoin, the risk is 10%. One is betting a tenth of the value of their portfolio on this investment.

My approach to risk encompasses all of the above, though the risk of the former definition can be reduced significantly by an understanding of the latter.

Before I get into the details of this all, however, I'd like to reiterate a comment I've made numerous times in this book: please refrain from beginning your trading journey with money that you cannot afford to lose. The most bulletproof risk management strategy of all-time won't be able to help you if you're investing unexpendable capital. There is an emotional trauma that embeds itself in the mind when one experiences the loss of money that is an absolute necessity for living, and the eradication of emotional decision-making is made infinitely easier simply by trading with disposable income. I began with a couple of hundred quid. This is the one financial space in the world where you truly can begin with next-to-nothing and realise life-changing gains, so, heed my advice and make the journey more pleasant for yourself. You'll find that everything else works out when you aren't under the constant stress of worrying about whether your underwater portfolio is on the cusp of getting you evicted from your home. You may even get a little sleep.

There is little to be said of the first definition of risk, in that I have already laid out the inherent volatility of the altcoins that we are most concerned with, namely, microcaps and lowcaps. These kinds of alts are obviously riddled with greater risks than their midcap or highcap counterparts, in the context of liquidity, but these greater risks are far outweighed by the upside available, especially when we develop a strategy to neutralise the extent of these by looking at the second definition. What I will say is something that may not be obvious to many in the space, especially those who have not been involved for all that long, and that is that, in my experience, microcaps and lowcaps are actually better coins to be positioned in in the event of a bear market. In a bear market, the surface-level safeties of the larger coins are fast dissolved, with this echelon of alts often experiencing the heaviest retracements. Meanwhile, microcaps and lowcaps are left relatively stable during these tumultuous periods, perhaps in part due to the lack of liquidity, forcing market-makers (and weak hands) to hold on to their positions. This is especially noticeable in the most fundamentally-solid lowcap projects.

All of that being said, you will, undoubtedly, experience greater volatility in your positions when pursuing the more alluring rewards of the smaller projects, and, as such, we do need to think about minimising the risks. Because of the very real prospect that a microcap might simply fade away and die during the period of investment, it makes little sense to throw 50% of your portfolio at one. What I like to do is take a fixed-risk approach to my altcoin portfolio, and by this I mean that every altcoin I accumulate will occupy a predetermined percentage of the value of my portfolio, with this percentage being dependent upon the circulating market cap of the coin. A caveat to this approach is the exclusion of highcaps – though I do not buy these very often at all, if and when I do, I like to use a stop-loss based on technical support and resistance levels. For microcaps, lowcaps and midcaps, I use fixed-risk, as follows:

- Microcaps: 0-1%
- Lowcaps: 1-3%
- Midcaps: 3-5%

To clarify, any microcaps I accumulate will occupy a maximum of 1% of the value of my altcoin portfolio, lowcaps will occupy a maximum of 3%, and midcaps a maximum of 5%. What fixed-risk also means is that the position will be held indefinitely with no stop-loss.

So, let's run through a quick example. Imagine I find a lowcap that looks promising and I have determined it to be trading at a solid entry price. I would accumulate an amount of it no greater than 3% of the bitcoin value of my altcoin portfolio at the time (and, in the case of multiple buys at different times, I use the figure for the portfolio's value at the time of the first buy). Then, this position is held until either, the coin begins to hit my sell targets and I can distribute my position, or, the coin plummets to zero and I lose the predetermined percentage of the value of my altcoin portfolio, not that this often happens. This way, I am aware of the maximum loss I can experience in the worst-case scenario without having to use a stop-loss, as stop-losses are absolutely useless in the extreme volatility of smaller projects.

This approach has been very effective and successful, in my experience, and allows for exposure to a greater number of potentially life-changing positions, whilst reducing the downside of each of those positions to a predetermined amount. We'll get into the specifics of how my portfolio is structured in the next section, but this approach to risk is also beneficial to your portfolio in bear markets, for the reasons I mentioned earlier: a portfolio comprised of, for example, fifty microcaps, lowcaps and midcaps spreads risk effectively whilst increasing exposure to projects with greater upside **and** minimising the depreciation of the value of the portfolio in a bear market, as microcaps and lowcaps experience less intense dumping during these periods. Think about it – particularly if you have researched the fundamentals and technicals of your investments sufficiently, the probability of **all** of these smaller projects becoming valueless is extremely slim, and the probability of finding a handful that grow exponentially is high. All you need is one 1% fixed-risk position growing 20x to potentially return 20% of the value of your portfolio and make up for the few that might not work out.

Portfolio: Portfolio management is a little bit more focused on numbers and specifics rather than some sort of investment philosophy, and, in truth, they are entirely experience-based. Below, I have written up a breakdown of the structure of my portfolio, and all I would say is that you tinker with the figures to suit your personal inclinations towards risk. I am particularly comfortable with high levels of risk – primarily because I continue to invest with money I can afford to lose (and experience, of course, helps) – as you will see from my altcoin portfolio structure, but for those who are less keen on greater exposure to riskier markets, just play about with this framework. Remember, this is exclusively an altcoin portfolio, which is why Bitcoin is not mentioned. My Bitcoin portfolio comprises of cold-storage and spare BTC for buying alts.

1. Highcaps: 10%. This tenth is predominantly used to actively trade the larger coins, though I tend to minimise my exposure here as much as possible, often dispersing this 10% across more midcaps, lowcaps and microcaps, as I no longer enjoy spending my time focused on short-term trading.

217

2. Midcaps: 25%. Here, I tend to scatter the quarter of the value of my portfolio between five to seven established projects, each occupying around 3-5% of my portfolio. These are larger positions, but I find that the higher level of liquidity available over microcaps and lowcaps justifies the increased exposure, despite the decreased potential upside.

3. Lowcaps and Microcaps: 65%. The bulk of my portfolio is positioned here for the reasons stated in the risk section. I won't repeat them here. Suffice to say, they provide the best opportunities.

All that this means is that around two-thirds of the value of my altcoin portfolio is usually positioned in anywhere from fifteen to fifty microcaps and lowcaps, with the other third being comprised of a handful of midcaps and maybe one or two highcaps. The reasoning behind this is simply that I am more confident in my abilities with the smaller projects than I am with their more-established counterparts. As I say, tinker with these figures, but I hope they provide you with a skeleton and point-of-reference for your own portfolios.

Market Psychology

Whilst technical analysis is my favourite mode of analysis, this section may well be my favourite in the entire book. There is little I find more fascinating that human psychology, and, after several years of watching the same patterns play out independent of the market that I'm observing, the reality of the constancy of our emotions has been cemented. Forget everything else, the chart that is printed below is one of the most important images to fix in your mind – and it's something you could've pulled for free on Google Images; sucks, I know.

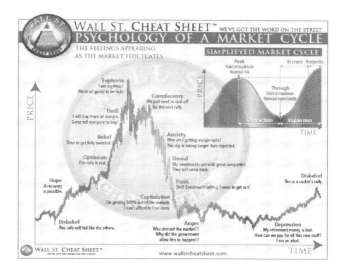

I have never seen an image so accurately and effectively represent market psychology and how it manifests in price-action. This *Wall St. Cheat Sheet* chart provides you with the framework for all market cycles, and market cycles are paramount. When coupled with comprehensive fundamental and technical analysis, an understanding of market cycles can make trading alts seem inconceivably straightforward. I think that a few examples wouldn't go amiss here to demonstrate exactly what I mean. Take a look at the handful of altcoin charts printed on the following pages and compare them to the *Wall St. Cheat Sheet*.

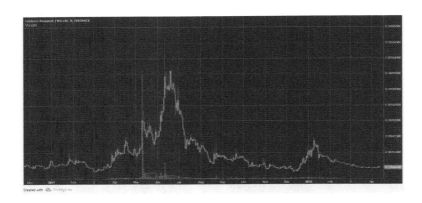

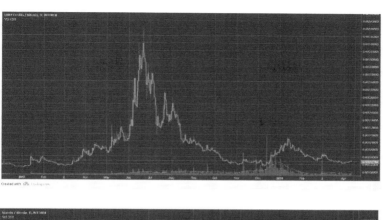

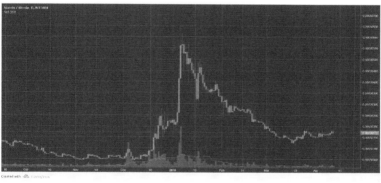

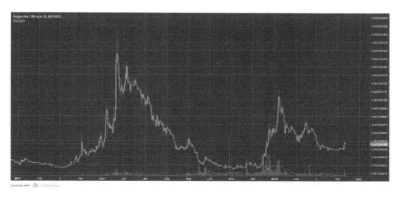

Now, I don't know about you, but the resemblance between them all and the *Wall St. Cheat Sheet* is uncanny; almost identical. Go through your favourite exchange and pick out a few more altcoins (that have at least twelve months of chart history). Now observe the same market cycles repeating themselves over and over again. One exercise that I found useful was to plot out the emotions of the cheat sheet on as many altcoin charts as possible – what this does primarily is train one's eye to spot these market cycles instantly, but it also develops one's ability to plot out a potential future trajectory. Take, for example, this chart for GRC, which I have annotated:

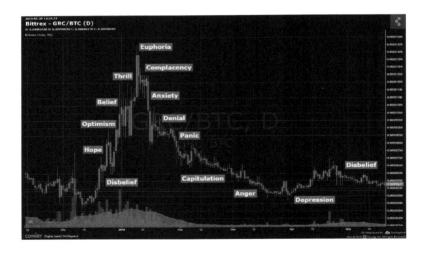

As you can see, the market cycle plays out perfectly. Whilst no one can legitimately predict the extent of future market cycles, this exercise gives us useful points-of-interest, perhaps acting as sell targets for our positions. I find it helpful to have this all mapped out, so that when price starts to move, I can reference it against the cheat sheet and get a rough idea of where we might be.

Market cycles are much faster in the cryptosphere than in any other financial market, and this is why I believe the cheat sheet is so effective: human psychology is constant, irrespective of the market, but the pace of the altcoin markets allows for these emotions to be observed (and felt) in an expedited manner, making them much more readily exploitable than in the slow, elongated market cycles found in more traditional markets. With alts, you really can take a glance at a chart and figure out roughly where the market cycle is, using that information for the accumulation and distribution of your positions. But what's the takeaway from this exercise in market psychology? Where specifically can this be implemented in your strategy?

Well, there is one rule I use relating to market cycles in my own strategy, and that is to **accumulate in depression.** This is pretty much the most bulletproof method to minimise downside and maximise upside for a trade, and it doesn't require any technical analysis at all. This harks back to the *Accumulation and Distribution* section, where I talked about channels of accumulation and how to spot them on the chart, and, of course, technical support will enhance the success of your accumulation and improve its efficiency, but it isn't a necessity. Simply look for fundamentally-sound projects that have already experienced a market cycle, await their descent into depression, and start buying. Take another look at that GRC chart, and then at all the other charts in this section. Anyone who bought during the multiple periods of depression on those charts had a profitable position shortly afterwards, with minimal time spent underwater. This is just a fact – and the magic – of market psychology. Given a sufficient time-frame, those who buy alts in 'depression' will experience successful trades, and **that** is exactly why the previous section on risk is so vital – it provides you with the opportunity for patience. When you know that your risk is predetermined, you can hold your position all the way from depression through euphoria with little concern. The beautiful thing is that, in this space, it really is that simple.

Chapter Five

THE PROCESS

And how exactly, I hear you ask, can one combine everything I've talked about in the book to create a concrete process for researching, accumulating and distributing altcoins? You're shit out of luck – I don't have one.

I'm just kidding, of course. There is a step-by-step process that I roughly follow for all new positions, and I figured it might be helpful for me to go through it here, so that you have a reference point to return to during the initial stages of your trading journey. Eventually, you will each fashion your own process, unique to your personalities and preferred style of speculation, but I know, for one, that having a rough framework with which to work would have been invaluable for me in the beginning.

As we have established in the preceding chapters of the book, there are three stages to each trade or investment: **research**; **accumulation**; **distribution** – or, the sourcing of an alt, the buying of that alt and the eventual selling of that alt. This chapter will sequentially work through these three stages. Without further ado, let's begin:

Research:

1. The research stage always begins by directing my browser to Coinmarketcap.

2. I click 'View All', and filter the list for microcaps and lowcaps using the Market Cap tab. This often must be done in separate stages, as CMC only allows for narrow, predetermined filtering. Nonetheless, the vast majority of the coins I focus my attention on are found within the $100k-$1mn filter.

3. I then filter for volume, choosing the $1k+ option. This removes many coins with little to no interest. The remaining coins are the ones that require further research.

4. I click through every single coin in this list, opening a new tab for each. If the list is too large, I will do this in batches to prevent my computer from frying...

5. I then go back and filter the coins using the other two potentially fruitful options in the Market Cap tab: $0-100k and $1mn-$10mn. I repeat steps 3 and 4, until I have a comprehensive list of all altcoins on CMC with a market cap under $10mn and trading volume over $1k. This is often well over 100 coins.

6. From this point, I go through each tab to determine which exchanges each coin trades on. You can do this by clicking the 'Markets' tab on each coin's individual page. If none of the exchanges I identified earlier in the book appear on the list (Binance; Bittrex; Poloniex; KuCoin; Livecoin; Cryptopia; CoinExchange; CryptoBridge), the tab is

closed. After whittling down the number of tabs, I write down the names of the remaining coins in a notebook. This is the 'further research' list.

7. Coin supply is the next port-of-call. Alongside the names of each coin, I write down its circulating supply, total supply and maximum supply. The preferred parameters from the earlier passage on coin supplies are used to further reduce the list. Coins with less than six-digit or greater than nine-digit circulating supplies are crossed off. I may still have 50 or more altcoins in contention at this point.

8. This is where I get into the nitty-gritty fundamental analysis, leaving Coinmarketcap and venturing into Bitcointalk threads and the like. As I mentioned earlier in the book, any coin without a Bitcointalk thread is as good as non-existent to me, so those are an instant delete from the list. I open up a tab for the Bitcointalk thread of those that remain. You can do this directly from Coinmarketcap to save you the trouble of finding the page yourself.

9. The first thing I am looking for from these threads is block parameters, reward structure and premine information. Inflation calculations are done for each and every coin, if this information is available. If it isn't, you know what to do (cross the coin off the list). These are all written up in the notebook with the corresponding coin. Refer back to the section on inflation if you've forgotten what these calculations are and what I am looking for from

them. The results provide a further means by which to reduce the list, as does the existence of a large premine or a premine of any size without justification. After these first nine steps, my list tends to be around 20-30 coins long, though sometimes it can be longer. All of the data being compiled in the notebook (or on a spreadsheet, if you prefer) will be what assists in intra-list comparison.

10. The remaining steps of the research process are all concerned with potential. I've established a list of coins that exhibit all of the preferred parameters, so the task is then to distinguish between these and figure out which coins have the greatest potential for growth. Community and development analysis, as explained in their own sections, are what I first tend to look at. I determine which coins have the strongest communities and social presences, and look at what the team have developed thus far and what they are envisioning for the project, noting all of this information down so that the process of cross-comparison is easier. Coins that come up weak are removed from the list.

11. The final step is to assess the block explorers of the remaining coins, investigating their rich-lists and distribution tabs for signs of smart-money accumulation. Ideally, the list of coins numbers around 10-15 by this stage. Rich-list evaluation prepares me for subsequent technical analysis and my own accumulation process. I don't remove any

coins from the list during this step, regardless of the data from the rich-lists. Just because there may not be clear-cut accumulation currently underway, doesn't mean there won't be, and given all of the prior fundamental analysis, I am confident that these remaining coins are all potential winners.

Accumulation:

1. The difficult part of the trade is over. If I've done my research thoroughly and effectively, the accumulation process should be one of little worry. The first step I take towards accumulating my own positions is determining a percentage of my capital to allocate to each coin, often dependent upon each coin's market cap and fundamental strength.

2. I then load up the charts for each of these coins and apply my technical analysis strategy, identifying long-term support levels and potential accumulation ranges that I might be able to fill my position within. I also look for accumulation spikes in the volume data, as well as attempting to determine where price is currently trading on the market cycle. I only ever buy during periods of 'anger' or 'depression'. Once I have determined a price range that I am keen on accumulating at (and an ideal average price for my position), I start setting orders up to the value of the predetermined percentage of my capital. If I am lucky enough to find large enough sell orders within my price range, I market buy those. This is rare, and the accumulation process often takes at least a week, if

not longer, before the position is filled. Sometimes, for microcaps or newer coins, I am forced to micro-buy (buy very small amounts) at market over a longer period of time in order to get a sizeable position at a price I consider optimal.

Distribution:

1. Distribution is more difficult to execute optimally than accumulation, but the process is simple enough. This entire stage of the trade is comprised of determining sell targets using Fibonacci extensions, horizontal resistance levels and the monitoring of rich-lists, orderbooks and the market cycle. Also, the value of each position is broken down into portions, with each portion being allocated to a different sell target. The predetermined sell targets and position portions are then written down, and alarms are set up at around 3-5% below each of these prices. Coins are stored, where possible, off exchanges, and as price begins to grow and approach these levels, the required portion of the position is transferred to the exchange to be sold.

That is pretty much the framework for every trade that I make. There are always exceptions and anomalies, but, for the most part, I approach every potential position using this three-stage process. Tinker with it to suit your own trading style, but make sure to spend copious amounts of effort and attention on the research stage, in particular. Accumulation and distribution will follow readily from thorough research.

Chapter Six

SECURITY

This next section is less of a chapter and more of a checklist, and whilst there are undoubtedly individuals in the space who have a more extensive and superior knowledge of security than me, I figured it might be worth writing up an easily digestible list of steps I take to secure myself, especially since so many have asked me to do so following the hack.

- First and foremost, download Bitdefender or a similar, high-level security suite for your PC.

- Get yourself a U2F key. This is a physical key that acts as a second layer of authentication, primarily for use with email accounts. Essentially, to log in to your email, you would need access to this key. Also, get yourself a spare – you can connect more than one key to your email accounts, so this will save you a disaster if you lose one.

- Use a different email account for each exchange (and social media platform) that you use.

- Set a different password for every email account, social media platform and exchange. Use a password manager (preferably one that does not use cloud storage) to make it a little easier to remember these. Set an exceptionally strong master password for the password manager, and store a couple of copies of this on paper in safe places.

- Pick up a couple of hardware wallets – either a Trezor or a Ledger – and use these whenever possible to store your cryptocurrencies. It makes sense to split your portfolio across a number of these devices if it is large enough to make it worthwhile. For storage of altcoins that aren't supported on a hardware wallet, either store them on a paper wallet or a local wallet on your PC. Store as little as possible on exchanges.

- On the above point, if it is necessary for a local wallet to be downloaded, run the file through VirusTotal prior to downloading and after downloading (sometimes I have seen different results for both these scans). Use the Sandbox function on your PC security suite to test-run the wallets the first time. If there are any issues that were not flagged initially by the VirusTotal scans, this will prevent the rest of your PC from being affected. In general, however, try to limit the number of local wallets you download for newer, less-established coins. These are more often than not the ones that might be problematic.

- For local wallets, ensure that you encrypt all of them with a strong, unique password. Either store these passwords in your password manager, or as physical copies (or both). Do not save copies of them anywhere else on your PC.

- For exchanges, utilise all of the available security measures. Every exchange worth its salt will allow for 2FA, so make sure this is enabled on all of them. Some exchanges also allow for IP Whitelisting (to prevent anyone logging in to your accounts from anywhere else) and Withdrawal Whitelisting (to prevent withdrawals to addresses not in your verified list).

- On the above point, **NEVER** use SMS 2FA for exchanges or email accounts. Use Google Authenticator or Authy instead, and ideally on a separate device that is not connected to the internet 24/7.

- Store backups of your wallet.dat files for local wallets and your 2FA secret keys for exchanges on an encrypted USB drive, and store that in a safe place.

- Use a Virtual Private Network (VPN) for all internet usage on any device associated with your cryptocurrencies.

Bibliography

- https://www.cheatsheet.com/money-career/your-cheat-sheet-to-the-psychology-of-market-cycles-infographic.html/

- http://www.theinnercircletrader.com/

- http://www.mnrank.com/

- http://www.masternodes.pro/

- http://www.tradingview.com

- http://www.coinigy.com

- https://chainz.cryptoid.info/blk/#!rich

- https://www.worldcoinindex.com/coin/dogecoin

- https://www.shieldx.sh/roadmap

- http://condensate.io/richlist

- https://medium.com/@daytradernik/picking-out-microcaps-101-2215a5782691

- https://steemit.com/bitcoin/@notsofast/4-ways-to-secure-your-bags-bitcoin-altcoins-cryptoasset-tokens-whatever-a-notsofast-security-primer

1Fk8TakmxzBYoaGEdMDqQwjxnrsFZK9pYK

Find me on Twitter: @cointradernik

https://www.altcointradershandbook.com

For those who'd like to see full-colour versions of the charts depicted in the book:
http://s000.tinyupload.com/index.php?
file_id=43368423681073584584

If you found the book amusing or insightful, I'd really appreciate it if you could leave a short Amazon or Goodreads review!

Printed in Poland
by Amazon Fulfillment
Poland Sp. z o.o., Wrocław

73406933R00132